The Regular Person Guide to Starting and Running a Non-Profit

Alfonzo "Al" Bailey, MPA

The Regular Person Guide to Starting and Running a Non-Profit

Copyright © 2026 by Alfonzo "Al" Bailey

All rights reserved. No part of this book may be reproduced or transmitted in any form or by any means without written permission from the author.

ISBN: 978-0-9890946-7-2

CONTENTS

Chapter 1: The Idea 1

Chapter 2: Your Options 8

Chapter 3: Honing the Idea 16

Chapter 4: Choosing Your Audience 24

Chapter 5: Putting Together the Board 31

Chapter 6: The Incorporation Paperwork 38

Chapter 7: Completing Your 501(c)(3) Application 43

Chapter 8: Creating the Program 50

Chapter 9: Setting Up Your Finances 65

Chapter 10: Finding Funding 75

Chapter 11: Building Your Team 88

Chapter 12: Keeping It Going 97

Appendices 106

CHAPTER 1: THE IDEA

"Every great thing starts with someone who simply decided to try."

You've got an idea. Maybe it keeps you up at night. Maybe it hits you every time you drive through a certain part of town, or every time you hear about another family going through the same mess you went through. Something inside you keeps saying, "Somebody should do something about this." And then, a little quieter, another voice chimes in: "Maybe that somebody is me."

If that sounds familiar, you're in the right place. Before we get into paperwork, tax-exempt status, boards of directors, or any of that stuff, we need to talk about the most important thing—your idea. Every nonprofit that's ever existed started right where you are now. One person. One observation. A feeling that wouldn't go away.

This chapter is about understanding your idea, testing whether it's got real potential, and building up enough confidence to actually move forward. We're going to have an honest talk about what might be holding you back and why those obstacles aren't nearly as big as they feel right now.

WHERE NONPROFIT IDEAS COME FROM

Here's something that might surprise you: nonprofit ideas don't come from business school textbooks or fancy boardrooms. They come from real life. From pain, frustration, love, and a stubborn refusal to accept that "this is just how things are." Let me give you some examples.

Personal experience is probably the most powerful source. Picture a parent whose kid struggled with a learning disability, and they spent years trying to find affordable tutoring that just wasn't there. After fighting the system for so long, that parent finally says, "I'm going to build the thing that should have existed for my family." The idea didn't come from a strategic plan. It came from sitting at a kitchen table, watching their child cry over homework, and thinking, "No other family should have to do this alone."

Sometimes it's about paying attention to what's happening around you. Maybe you volunteer at a food bank and you start noticing that most of the folks coming through the door are seniors who can't easily get to the grocery store. The food bank helps, sure, but nobody's dealing with the transportation piece. That little observation—"what if somebody organized a grocery delivery service for homebound seniors?"—that's a nonprofit idea.

Professional experience is another big one. Think about a social worker who's spent fifteen years in the child welfare system and keeps seeing the same gaps. Kids aging out of foster care with no life skills, no support network, no clue how to rent an apartment or set up a bank account. After seeing it happen enough times, that social worker says, "I know exactly what these kids need, and I'm going to build it."

And then there are the ideas that come from crisis. A community gets rocked by a string of overdose deaths, or a natural disaster, or a spike in youth violence, and somebody steps up and says, "We can't sit around waiting for someone else to handle this." That urgency, that refusal to look the other way—that's where a lot of nonprofit missions are born.

Whatever your version of this looks like, the common thread is pretty simple: you see a gap between what is and what should be, and something in you says, "I'm going to try to close it." That feeling isn't random. It's the beginning of something real.

MEET LISA: A STORY OF AN IDEA TAKING SHAPE

Let me introduce you to someone we're going to spend a lot of time with in this book. Her name is Lisa. She's not a real person—but her story is stitched together from the experiences of dozens of real people I've worked with over the years. She represents the kind of person who picks up a book like this one.

Lisa's forty-two. She works as an office manager at a small insurance company in a mid-sized city. Two kids, a mortgage, a car payment—the whole deal. She didn't study nonprofit management in college. She doesn't have a trust fund or a bunch of wealthy friends on speed dial. What she does have is a problem she can't stop thinking about.

Three years back, Lisa's teenage daughter went through a serious mental health crisis. Finding affordable counseling? A nightmare. Waiting lists stretched for months. The few places that took their insurance were swamped. Lisa spent weeks making calls, driving an hour each way to appointments, and arguing with insurance companies. Her daughter eventually got help, but the whole ordeal left scars on the entire family.

Since then, Lisa's been talking to other parents who went through the same thing. She's shown up at school board meetings where parents are practically begging for more mental health resources. She reads the articles. She feels the frustration building. Then one night, sitting at her kitchen table after yet another phone call with a parent who doesn't know where to turn, she grabs a napkin and scribbles: "What if there was a place where families could get mental health help without jumping through a million hoops?"

That napkin note? That's Lisa's nonprofit idea. It's not a business plan. It's barely even a complete thought. But it's the seed of something that could genuinely change lives in her community.

We're going to follow Lisa through every chapter of this book. You'll watch her wrestle with the same questions you're probably asking right now. And you'll see her figure it out—not because she's got some special talent, but because she's willing to learn and she refuses to quit.

THE FEARS THAT HOLD PEOPLE BACK

Alright, before we go any further, let's deal with the elephant in the room. You're probably scared. Good. I'd honestly be a little worried if you weren't. Starting a nonprofit is a big deal. But here's what I've learned after years of helping people launch organizations: the fears that stop most people are built on myths, not reality. Let's knock them down one at a time.

"I'm Not Qualified"

This is the big one, and I hear it constantly. People think starting a nonprofit requires a special degree, or a background in finance, or twenty years of experience running organizations. It doesn't. Some of the most impactful nonprofits in this country were started by people who had zero formal training in any of this stuff.

Think about it. Who's more qualified to start a recovery program—somebody with an MBA who's never experienced addiction, or a person who spent ten years getting sober and now spends their weekends helping others do the same? Credentials have their place, but in the nonprofit world, passion, lived experience, and sheer determination count for just as much. Often more.

Now look—that doesn't mean you won't need to learn things. You absolutely will. That's what this book is for. But don't confuse "I've got some learning to do" with "I'm not the right person for this." Every nonprofit founder starts as a beginner. The ones who make it are the ones who stay curious and keep asking questions.

"I Don't Have Any Money"

Here's a secret: most nonprofits don't start with a pile of cash. They start with sweat equity, borrowed conference rooms, and donated supplies. This idea that you need tens of thousands of dollars before you can even get going? One of the biggest myths out there.

Will you eventually need funding? Absolutely. Running an organization costs money. But you don't need a dime to start developing your idea, making connections, or laying groundwork. Plenty of founders start by volunteering their time, pulling together small community gatherings, and building momentum long before they file a single piece of paperwork. We'll get deep into the money side later. For now, just hear me: being broke is a challenge to work through, not a reason to give up before you've started.

"I Don't Know the Right People"

You might not know them yet. But you will. And honestly, building a network happens more naturally than you'd think once you start talking about your idea with some genuine fire behind it. People gravitate toward people who care deeply about something. When you start sharing your vision—at community meetings, at church, at your kid's school, even on social media—you'll be surprised at who steps forward.

When Lisa started talking about her idea at a parent-teacher meeting, another mom mentioned her brother-in-law was an attorney who did free work for nonprofits. A coworker overheard Lisa chatting about her plans over lunch and volunteered to build a website. That's how it works. You put the idea out there, and connections start appearing in places you didn't expect. You don't need a packed rolodex on day one. You just need to open your mouth and start talking.

"What If I Fail?"

This one deserves the most honest answer I can give you. Ready? You might fail. Some nonprofits don't make it. Some ideas don't pan out the way you hoped. That's the truth, and I'm not going to sugarcoat it.

But here's what I want you to sit with: what's the cost of not trying? If Lisa never starts her organization, those families in her community still don't have a way to get their kids into mental health services. The problem doesn't disappear just because she was too afraid to act. And even if her first shot doesn't land exactly the way she pictured, the experience she picks up, the relationships she builds, the awareness she raises—all of that still has value. Failure in the nonprofit world is rarely a dead end. Organizations that close their doors often leave behind programs, partnerships, and seeds that somebody else picks up and grows.

The real failure? That's never trying at all.

HOW TO TEST YOUR IDEA

Okay, so you've got your idea and you've decided fear isn't going to run the show. Good for you. But before you sprint to the computer and start Googling "how to start a nonprofit," pump the brakes for a minute. You need to spend some time testing your idea first. And I'm not talking about some formal market study or a hundred-page business plan. I'm talking about asking yourself a few honest questions—and actually listening to the answers.

WHAT PROBLEM AM I ACTUALLY SOLVING?

Sounds obvious, right? You'd be amazed how many people struggle with this one. "I want to help people" is a beautiful intention, but it's not a problem statement. Now compare that to: "Families in my county can't get their kids into mental health services because there are only two providers who take Medicaid, and both have six-month waitlists." See the difference? One is a feeling. The other is something you can actually build a program around.

Sit down and write out the problem you want to solve. Be specific. Who's affected? Roughly how many people? What happens to them because this problem isn't getting fixed? What's already out there, and why isn't it working? The sharper your problem statement, the stronger everything else will be.

IS SOMEBODY ELSE ALREADY DOING THIS?

Critical question. If another organization in your community is already doing exactly what you've got in mind, that doesn't automatically mean you should pack it in. But it does mean you need to think hard about what makes your approach different—or whether teaming up with them might be smarter than starting something brand new.

Do your homework. Search online. Call the local United Way or community foundation and ask what they know about organizations in your space. If you find someone doing great work on your issue, maybe volunteer with them first. You might realize that a partnership gets you further than going solo. Or you might discover their approach leaves a gap that your idea fills perfectly.

Lisa dug around and found a few mental health providers in her area, but none of them were focused on helping families actually navigate the system and connect with affordable services. The gap was real, and her idea addressed it head-on.

DOES ANYBODY ELSE CARE ABOUT THIS?

A nonprofit is, by definition, a community effort. You can't pull this off alone, and frankly, you shouldn't want to. So ask yourself: who else is affected by this problem? Who else gets frustrated about it? Who would actually show up if you invited them to talk about solutions?

Start having those conversations. Talk to friends, neighbors, coworkers, people at church. Share your idea and watch how people react. If you keep hearing, "I've been saying the same thing for years!" or "My family dealt with that exact situation"—that's a strong signal. If you're mostly getting polite nods and blank stares, you might need to rethink your approach.

Lisa started by reaching out to parents she'd met during her daughter's crisis. She threw together an informal coffee meetup and invited a handful of them. Eight showed up. Then twelve. Then twenty. Every person brought a story and a hunger for change. The community was telling her loud and clear: this matters.

AM I ACTUALLY WILLING TO COMMIT TO THIS?

Real talk: starting a nonprofit is not a weekend project. It takes sustained effort, patience, and the grit to keep pushing when things get hard—and they will get hard. Before you go any further, be honest with yourself about whether you're really ready for that kind of commitment.

You don't have to quit your job tomorrow. Lots of founders build their organizations nights and weekends while keeping a full-time paycheck. But you do need to be realistic about your bandwidth. Can you carve out five hours a week? Ten? Do you have people in your life who'll back you up and share the load when things get heavy?

Lisa knew she couldn't walk away from her day job. But she also knew she could give her evenings and weekends to something that mattered this much. She sat her family down, told them what she was thinking, and got their support. She didn't have unlimited time. But she had enough to get started, and that was all she needed.

MOVING FROM IDEA TO ACTION

If you've made it this far, I'm guessing your idea held up. You can describe the problem clearly. There's a genuine gap in your community. Other people share your frustration. And you're willing to do the work. So what now?

Here's your next move, and it's simpler than you think: write it down. Not on a napkin this time. Grab a notebook or open up a blank document and put these five things on paper. First, the problem you want to tackle—two or three clear sentences. Second, who's affected. Third, what your solution looks like, even if it's rough. Fourth, why you're the right person to lead this. Fifth, what you still need to learn.

Nobody's grading this. It's for you. It's a way of pulling the idea out of your head and giving it some shape on the page. There's something that shifts when you write things down. The idea stops being a daydream and starts feeling like a plan.

Lisa did this one night after the kids went to bed. For the problem, she wrote: "Families in our community—especially those on Medicaid or without insurance—can't get timely mental health help for their kids. The waits are ridiculous, and most parents have no idea how to work the system." For who's affected: "Low and middle-income families with kids dealing with anxiety, depression, and other mental health struggles." For her solution: "A community organization that connects families to mental health resources, helps them navigate the process, and pushes for better access." Why her: "Because I lived it. I know exactly what these families are going through." What she needs to learn: "Basically everything in this book."

That kind of raw honesty is exactly what this stage calls for. You don't need perfect answers. You just need to be clear about the questions and willing to figure the rest out as you go.

YOU'RE MORE READY THAN YOU THINK

I want to leave you with something you might not fully believe yet: you're more ready than you think. Picking up this book and getting this far? That's already the hardest part—deciding you want to try. Everything that comes after—the legal stuff, the finances, building a board, raising money—that's all learnable. It's just steps in a process. And this book is going to walk you through every single one.

You don't need to be an expert. You don't need to be rich. You don't need to be best friends with the mayor or the head of some big foundation. What you need is a clear idea, a real desire to help, and the willingness to put in the work. If you've got those three things, you've got everything you need to start.

Here's what's coming next: in Chapter 2, we're going to hit pause and ask a question that might surprise you—whether starting a nonprofit is actually the right move for what you want to accomplish. Turns out, there are other options worth considering, and I want to make sure you pick the path that's genuinely best for your mission, not just the most obvious one. But before you flip that page, do me a favor. Tonight, or this weekend, sit down and write out those five things I mentioned. Treat it like a conversation with yourself. Be honest. Be specific. Don't worry about getting it perfect.

Your idea matters. The people you want to help are real. And the organization you're going to build? It starts right here, with you deciding this is worth doing.

Let's get to work.

The Regular Person Guide
CHAPTER 2: YOUR OPTIONS

"Just because you want to do good doesn't mean you have to start a nonprofit."

If you finished Chapter 1 feeling fired up and ready to go, good. That energy's going to serve you well. But before you start Googling "how to file for 501(c)(3) status," I need you to pump the brakes for just a minute. Because here's something most books about nonprofits won't tell you up front: starting a nonprofit isn't always the best way to solve a problem.

I know—that's a weird thing to read in a book called The Regular Person Guide to Starting and Running a Non-Profit. But I've seen too many well-meaning people rush into creating an organization when there were simpler, faster, and honestly more effective ways to accomplish what they wanted. Starting a nonprofit is a serious commitment. Legal obligations, financial responsibilities, ongoing work that most people don't fully grasp until they're already neck-deep in it.

So before we go any further, I want to make sure you understand all your options. We're going to look at the alternatives, break down what a 501(c)(3) actually is (and isn't), lay out the real benefits alongside the real downsides, and help you make a smart decision about whether forming your own organization is truly the right move.

DO YOU ACTUALLY NEED A NONPROFIT?

Let me put this as plainly as I can. A nonprofit is a tool. It's one specific way to organize people and resources around a cause. But it's not the only way, and it's not always the best way. The question you should be asking isn't "How do I start a nonprofit?" It's "What's the most effective way to solve this problem?"

Sometimes the answer is a nonprofit. Sometimes it's something else entirely. Here are five alternatives worth considering seriously.

VOLUNTEER WITH AN EXISTING ORGANIZATION

This is the option most people skip right past, and it's often the smartest place to start. Before you build something from scratch, find out if someone's already built something similar. There might be an organization in your community working on the same problem. Maybe they're underfunded or understaffed or just not reaching the right people. But they've got the infrastructure, the legal status, and the experience. What they might need is somebody like you—somebody with fire in their belly and fresh ideas.

Here's what volunteering gets you that's hard to get any other way: you learn how a nonprofit actually operates from the inside. The day-to-day reality of running programs, managing money, dealing with funders. That education is priceless, and it's free. Plus, you can start making an impact right away instead of spending months on setup. You might even discover that your idea fits naturally under their umbrella, which means you could launch your program without creating a whole separate entity.

Lisa did exactly this. Before diving into the nonprofit formation process, she spent time volunteering at a small family services agency that did some mental health referrals. Within a few weeks she was helping families find resources and getting a front-row seat to how the agency ran. She learned a ton—and she also confirmed that there really was a gap that her idea could fill. That volunteer experience became the foundation for everything she built afterward.

FISCAL SPONSORSHIP

This one's underused and I wish more people knew about it. A fiscal sponsorship is basically an arrangement where an established nonprofit agrees to be the legal and financial home for your project. You get to do your work, raise money, and run your program without having to create your own nonprofit from scratch.

Here's how it works in practice. You find a nonprofit with 501(c)(3) status whose mission lines up with yours. You pitch them on sponsoring your project. If they say yes, donations to your project flow through their organization—so donors still get their tax deductions. The sponsor handles the legal and financial stuff: tax returns, bank accounts, IRS compliance. In exchange, they take a small cut, usually somewhere between five and fifteen percent. You get to focus on the actual work.

Think of fiscal sponsorship as a test drive. You can build your program, raise some money, serve people, and see if the concept has legs—all without the cost and complexity of incorporating and filing for tax-exempt status. If things take off, you can always spin off into your own nonprofit later. If they don't? You haven't sunk thousands of dollars into an organization that never got traction.

Lisa looked into this seriously. She found a community health organization willing to sponsor her navigation project, and it would've let her start serving families right away. She ultimately went a different direction, but she kept it in her back pocket as a backup. For a lot of you reading this, fiscal sponsorship might actually be the perfect starting point.

JUST GATHER SOME PEOPLE AND DO THE WORK

Not every good deed needs a legal entity behind it. Sometimes the most effective thing you can do is round up some people who care and start doing the work. No articles of incorporation. No board of directors. No tax-exempt status. Just people showing up.

This works best when the effort is relatively small, doesn't need major funding, and is focused on direct action. A neighborhood cleanup crew. Parents who organize free tutoring at the library every Tuesday. A group of volunteers who visit nursing homes on weekends. These are meaningful, real things that don't require a formal organizational structure.

The trade-off? Without formal status, you can't offer tax-deductible receipts to donors, you can't apply for most grants, and you can't enter into contracts as an organization. But if your goal is to make an immediate difference with what you've already got, an informal group can be incredibly powerful. And if things grow to the point where you need more structure, you can always formalize later.

START A SOCIAL ENTERPRISE

A social enterprise is a business that exists to solve a social problem. Unlike a traditional nonprofit, it makes money by selling products or services. Unlike a regular business, social impact is the whole point—not maximizing profit for owners.

Examples are everywhere once you start looking. A coffee shop that employs people transitioning out of homelessness. A landscaping company that hires and trains formerly incarcerated workers. An app that connects volunteers with local organizations and charges a small subscription fee to keep the lights on.

The big advantage here is self-sufficiency. Instead of being on a perpetual fundraising treadmill, you generate your own revenue. The downside is that you're running a business, with all the headaches that come along with it—competition, pricing, cash flow, marketing. It's a great option if your idea naturally lends itself to a business model, but it's not the right fit for every type of community need.

PARTNER WITH AN ESTABLISHED NONPROFIT

This goes a step beyond volunteering. Instead of just giving your time, you approach an existing nonprofit and propose running a specific program under their organizational umbrella. You get their legal structure, financial systems, and credibility. They get a new program and a passionate person to run it.

It can work beautifully. It's faster and cheaper than starting from scratch, and it lets you focus on serving people instead of building bureaucratic infrastructure. The downside is you don't have full control—you're operating within somebody else's organization, which means playing by their rules. If you care more about getting things done than having your name on the door, though, this can be an excellent path.

SO WHAT EXACTLY IS A 501(C)(3)?

Alright, you've looked at the alternatives and you still think starting your own nonprofit is the move. Good—but before you take that step, let's make sure you actually understand what you're signing up for. The term "501(c)(3)" gets thrown around like confetti, but most people don't really know what it means.

Here's the short version. A 501(c)(3) is a type of organization recognized by the IRS—the Internal Revenue Service. The name comes from the specific section of the federal tax code that defines organizations exempt from paying federal income tax: Section 501, subsection (c), paragraph (3). Basically, the government has looked at your organization and said, "You exist to serve a charitable, educational, religious, or scientific purpose, so we're not going to tax you on the money you bring in."

But here's what trips people up: a 501(c)(3) isn't just a tax break. It's a legal commitment to operate in a very specific way. You're telling the government and the public that your organization exists to serve the common good—not to make money for the people who run it. That distinction matters, and it comes with a long list of rules about how you raise money, spend money, and report what you're doing.

Quick note on categories: there are two main types of 501(c)(3) organizations—public charities and private foundations. Most of what people picture when they hear "nonprofit"—community health centers, food banks, mentoring programs, after-school organizations—those are public charities. They're funded by lots of different sources: individual donors, grants, government contracts. Private foundations are usually funded by a single source, like a wealthy family. For this book, we're focused on public charities, because that's what most of you will be building.

WHAT TAX-EXEMPT ACTUALLY MEANS (AND DOESN'T MEAN)

People hear "tax-exempt" and think it means you never deal with taxes. Not quite. It means your organization doesn't pay federal income tax on money that comes in related to your mission. A hundred thousand in donations? No income tax owed. A food bank selling donated goods at low cost? Those revenues generally aren't taxed either.

But you're not off the hook entirely. You still pay payroll taxes for employees, just like any other employer. You might owe state sales taxes depending on where you operate. And if your nonprofit earns money from something unrelated to your mission—say your mentoring organization opens a car wash on the side—that income can get hit with what's called "unrelated business income tax."

The other huge piece: 501(c)(3) status means people who donate to you can deduct those gifts on their personal taxes. This matters more than you might think. A lot of donors—and nearly all foundations and corporations—want to know their contributions are tax-deductible before they'll write a check. Without that status, you're locked out of a significant chunk of the funding landscape.

THE REAL BENEFITS OF FORMING A 501(C)(3)

Now that you know what a 501(c)(3) is, let's talk about why so many people go this route. There are some genuinely powerful advantages.

Tax-deductible donations are the obvious one. When donors know their gifts reduce their tax bill, they're more willing to give—and they tend to give bigger. Major donors, family foundations, corporate sponsors—almost all of them require 501(c)(3) status before they'll even look at you.

Then there's grant access. The vast majority of grants from private foundations, government agencies, and corporate giving programs are only open to registered 501(c)(3) organizations. Want to apply for funding from your state government or your local community foundation? You'll need tax-exempt status to even be eligible.

Credibility is the less tangible benefit, but it's real. Having a formal nonprofit structure tells potential partners, funders, and the public that you're serious and accountable. You've got a board providing oversight. You're filing public reports. That legitimacy opens doors to partnerships, media coverage, and community trust that informal efforts just can't access as easily.

And there's permanence. A nonprofit is designed to outlast any single person. A volunteer group might dissolve when the leader moves away. A properly structured nonprofit has a board, a mission, and a legal identity that can keep going even when the founder steps back. If you're building for the long haul, that structure matters.

Lisa saw all of this clearly. She wanted to apply for grants from the county mental health board. She needed schools and healthcare providers to take her seriously as a referral partner. And she wanted what she was building to last well beyond her own involvement. For her, the benefits made the decision straightforward.

THE REAL DOWNSIDES YOU NEED TO KNOW ABOUT

Here's where I need to be completely straight with you, because too many nonprofit guides gloss over this part. Forming and running a 501(c)(3) comes with real costs, real work, and real restrictions. Go in with your eyes open and you'll be fine. Ignore this stuff and it'll catch up with you.

Paperwork and compliance. From the moment you incorporate, you're dealing with forms, filings, and deadlines. Articles of incorporation with the state. A detailed IRS application that can take months to process. Annual returns even though you're tax-exempt. State registrations. Possibly local requirements too. Miss a filing deadline and you could lose your tax-exempt status. It's not impossible to manage, but it's not nothing either.

You don't own the organization. This one catches a lot of founders off guard. A nonprofit doesn't have owners. It's governed by a board of directors, and even though you started the thing, the board has ultimate legal authority. You can't treat the nonprofit's money as your personal piggy bank. You can't make every decision by yourself. And if things go sideways with your board, they could technically remove you from the organization you created. I'll say a lot more about boards later, but for now, understand that starting a nonprofit means sharing control.

Restrictions on how you operate. A 501(c)(3) can't get involved in political campaigns. It can only do limited lobbying. It can't distribute profits to anyone—no shareholders, no dividends, no bonuses from leftover funds. Every dollar has to go toward the mission. If the organization ever shuts down, the remaining assets go to another nonprofit—not back to you. These rules exist for good reasons, but they can feel constraining if you're used to calling all the shots.

Cost. You don't need a fortune to get started, but there are real expenses. State filing fees, IRS application fees, possible legal and accounting costs, insurance, ongoing operations. A lot of new nonprofits underestimate these numbers and find themselves scrambling to cover basics before they've served their first client.

Lisa wasn't scared off by any of this, but she didn't brush it aside either. She started a file tracking every requirement, deadline, and cost she'd need to deal with. No surprises—that was her approach, and it should be yours too.

MAKING YOUR DECISION

So how do you decide? Here's a simple way to think about it. A 501(c)(3) probably makes sense if your idea needs ongoing funding from grants and major donors, if you want to build something that lasts beyond your personal involvement, if you need institutional credibility to partner with schools, hospitals, or government agencies, and if you're prepared for the legal and financial obligations that come with the territory.

One of the alternatives probably makes more sense if your idea is small-scale and doesn't need significant funding, if you want to test your concept before going all in, if you're more interested in direct action than organization-building, or if there's an existing nonprofit that could house your program more effectively than a brand-new one could.

There's no shame in choosing a simpler path. Honestly, it takes more wisdom to pick the right tool for the job than to automatically grab the most complicated one. Some of the best community work I've ever seen was done by informal groups of dedicated people who never filed a single form with the IRS.

WHAT LISA DECIDED

Lisa took about two weeks to think it through. She volunteered with that family services agency and learned a lot. She explored fiscal sponsorship and even had a sit-down with a potential sponsor organization. She considered whether a simple volunteer group could get the job done.

In the end, she went with the 501(c)(3). Her reasons were clear: she wanted to go after government grants for mental health navigation services. She needed schools to take her seriously as a referral partner. She wanted to build something that would serve families for decades—not just as long as she personally had the bandwidth to keep showing up. And she was willing to take on the paperwork, the compliance, the board-building, because the mission was worth all of it.

But notice something about how Lisa handled this. She didn't rush. She took the time to understand her options, weigh the trade-offs, and make a deliberate choice. That kind of thoughtfulness is what separates founders who build something lasting from the ones who burn out in year two.

In Chapter 3, we're going to roll up our sleeves and get specific. You'll learn how to take that big, broad idea of yours and sharpen it into something focused and actionable—a clear problem statement, a defined population, a concrete solution, and a mission statement that actually means something. This is where your napkin scribble starts becoming a real organization. It's also where I'm going to introduce you to Marcus, whose cautionary tale about trying to solve every problem at once is something every aspiring founder needs to hear.

Whatever you decide about the path forward, make sure it's a decision—not just an assumption. Your community deserves your best thinking. So do you.

The Regular Person Guide
CHAPTER 3: HONING THE IDEA

"If you try to help everybody, you end up helping nobody."

You've got an idea. You've decided a nonprofit is the right vehicle for it. Now comes the part that a lot of founders skip—and later wish they hadn't. You need to take that big, broad idea and sharpen it into something specific, focused, and actionable. You need to go from "I want to help people" to "Here's exactly who I'm going to help, how I'm going to do it, and what changes when I succeed."

I can't stress this enough: the work in this chapter shapes everything that follows. Your mission statement will show up in your legal documents. Your vision will drive your fundraising pitches. Your values will influence who you hire and how your community sees you. Getting this right doesn't guarantee success, but skipping it—or faking your way through it—almost guarantees confusion, mission drift, and burnout down the road.

So grab a pen. This chapter isn't just reading—it's doing. I'm going to walk you through exercises that take the raw material of your idea and turn it into a real foundation for your organization.

THE PROBLEM WITH TRYING TO DO EVERYTHING

I need to tell you about Marcus. Marcus grew up in a tough neighborhood and watched his community get battered by poverty, violence, bad schools, no healthcare, unemployment, and drug addiction. When he decided to start a nonprofit, his concept was ambitious: he wanted to fix the whole neighborhood. After-school tutoring. Job training. A health clinic. Food pantry. Youth mentoring. Drug rehab. Community garden. All of it, all at once.

Marcus had a huge heart. He also had an impossible plan. When he tried to explain his organization to potential supporters, their eyes glazed over. Grant applications? Funders couldn't figure out what box to put him in. Programs? He and his tiny team were spread so thin that nothing got done well. Eighteen months in, Marcus was exhausted, broke, and ready to walk away.

Here's the thing—Marcus didn't fail because he was a bad leader or because his community didn't need help. He failed because he tried to solve every problem at once instead of picking one and solving it well. This is one of the most common traps for new founders, and it comes from a genuinely good place. When you care deeply about a community, narrowing your focus feels like abandoning people. But the reality is exactly the opposite. When you try to do everything, you accomplish nothing. When you pick one thing and do it exceptionally well, you build something that can grow over time.

Lisa felt this pull too. Her core idea was connecting families with mental health services, but the more people she talked to, the more needs she heard about—transportation to appointments, tutoring for kids who'd fallen behind, counseling for the parents themselves. Every request tugged at her. But a mentor had told her Marcus's story, and it stuck with her. She was going to start with one thing and do it right. Everything else could come later.

EXERCISE ONE: DEFINE THE PROBLEM

Time to get specific. Write out the problem you're trying to solve in no more than three sentences. The catch: every sentence has to include real details. No vague language. No buzzwords. Just an honest description of what's broken and who it's hurting.

Here's what vague looks like: "There's a mental health crisis affecting families in our community, and people need more resources and support to get the help they deserve." That sentence is technically true, but it tells nobody anything useful. It could describe any community in America. You can't design a program around it. You can't write a grant with it. It's wallpaper.

Now here's specific: "In Franklin County, families with children who need mental health services face wait times of four to six months for a provider who accepts Medicaid. Most parents don't know what services exist and can't navigate the referral process on their own. As a result, kids' conditions worsen, leading to school failures, family crises, and emergency room visits that could've been prevented."

See the difference? The second version tells you where, who, what the barrier is, and what happens when nobody fixes it. It paints a picture. It gives you something to build on.

Your turn. Write your problem statement. Be specific about the geography, the people, the nature of the problem, and the consequences.

If you don't have all the data yet, write what you know and make a note to research the rest. But don't hide behind vague language. Specificity is your friend here.

EXERCISE TWO: IDENTIFY YOUR PEOPLE

Every nonprofit serves a specific group of people. You might call them clients, participants, beneficiaries—whatever feels right. The label doesn't matter. What matters is that you know exactly who they are.

Create a detailed picture: age range, income level, where they live, family situation, and the specific challenges they're dealing with. The more detailed this gets, the better you'll be at designing programs that actually fit their lives.

Lisa's description: "Families in Franklin County with children ages five to eighteen experiencing mental health challenges—anxiety, depression, behavioral issues, trauma. These are mostly low to moderate income families, many on Medicaid or uninsured. A lot of the parents are working one or two jobs and just don't have the time or know-how to navigate a complicated healthcare system."

Look at what that does. It defines the kids' age range. It names the conditions. It pins down the economic reality. It explains why these particular families can't just solve this on their own. With that level of detail, Lisa can design a program that speaks directly to these families. She's not trying to serve everyone—she's serving a specific group with specific challenges, and she's going to serve them really well.

Write yours. And don't feel guilty about narrowing the focus. You're not saying other people don't matter. You're saying these are the people you're uniquely positioned to help right now. That's not exclusion. That's strategy.

EXERCISE THREE: DESCRIBE YOUR SOLUTION

You know the problem. You know who's affected. Now—what are you actually going to do about it? Describe your solution in practical, concrete terms. Not philosophy. Not theory. What does your organization do on a random Tuesday afternoon?

This is where a lot of aspiring founders stall out. They're crystal clear on what they're against—the problem—but fuzzy on what they're for.

"Raising awareness" isn't a solution. "Providing resources" is too vague to mean anything. You need to describe activities that lead somewhere.

Here's what Lisa wrote: "We'll run a family mental health navigation program. When a family contacts us, a trained navigator assesses their needs, identifies providers who accept their insurance or offer sliding-scale fees, helps them with the referral paperwork, and follows up to make sure they actually got connected to services. We'll also host monthly workshops at community locations to educate parents about kids' mental health, chip away at stigma, and point families toward resources. The goal is to cut the time from a family's first call to their first appointment from months to weeks."

Notice what she did there. She didn't describe some vague support service. She laid out a specific process: intake, assessment, provider matching, paperwork help, follow-up. She added a second piece—the workshops—that supports the core program. And she named a measurable goal: months to weeks. A funder reading this knows exactly what their money pays for. A family hearing about it knows what to expect. A volunteer knows what they'd be doing.

Write yours with that same level of detail. What activities will your organization do? What's the process someone goes through when they walk in your door? What's different in their life when they walk out?

WRITING A MISSION STATEMENT THAT ACTUALLY MEANS SOMETHING

If you've done the three exercises above, you've already got the raw material for your mission statement. A mission statement is one sentence—two at most—that captures who you serve, what you do, and why it matters. It's the most important sentence your organization will ever produce, because everything else flows from it.

The problem with most mission statements is they're written to sound impressive instead of being useful. You've seen the type: "We empower communities through innovative, holistic approaches to systemic change, fostering resilience and promoting equity across diverse populations." That sentence means absolutely nothing. It could describe a thousand different organizations. It's big words masking the absence of a clear idea.

A good mission statement is the opposite of that. It's clear, specific, and written so your grandmother could understand it. Here's a formula that works: "[Organization name] [what you do] for [who you serve] so that [why it matters]." That's it. Nothing fancy.

Lisa's: "The Family Bridge Project connects Franklin County families with affordable mental health services for their children by providing personalized navigation support, so that no family has to face the mental health system alone."

Read that out loud. You know instantly what the organization does, who it helps, and what difference it makes. No jargon. No fluff. A stranger reading it for the first time immediately gets what The Family Bridge Project is about.

A couple more examples to show the formula in action. A literacy org: "Reading First helps adults in the Riverside community learn to read and write through free, one-on-one tutoring, so that every adult has the skills to support their family and participate fully in their community." A housing nonprofit: "Safe Haven provides transitional housing and life skills training for young adults aging out of foster care in Metro City, so they can build stable, independent lives."

Three questions. What do you do? Who for? Why does it matter? If your mission statement answers all three in plain language, you're there. If it takes more than two sentences or needs a dictionary, simplify.

CRAFTING YOUR VISION STATEMENT

Your mission describes what you do right now. Your vision describes the future you're working toward. If the mission is the road, the vision is the destination.

A vision statement should be aspirational but believable. Not a fantasy—a genuine possibility your work is moving toward. Short, memorable, and a little bit dreamy. This is where you get to paint a picture of what the world looks like when your work succeeds.

Lisa's: "A community where every family can access the mental health support their children need, when they need it, without barriers."

Simple. Powerful. It describes a world that doesn't exist yet but one Lisa believes her work can help create. On the hard days—and there will be plenty—this is the sentence that reminds her why she's doing all of it.

Other examples: "A city where no child goes to bed hungry." "A world where every foster youth has the support they need to thrive as an adult." "A community where every person can read, write, and fully participate in civic life."

Notice these don't describe programs or activities. They describe the result of all those programs and activities. Your mission tells people what you do. Your vision tells people why it's worth doing. Aim for one or two sentences. Bold enough to inspire, grounded enough to feel achievable.

DEFINING YOUR VALUES

Mission says what you do. Vision says where you're headed. Values say how you'll get there. They're the principles that guide your organization's behavior, decisions, and culture—how you treat the people you serve, the people on your team, and the community you operate in.

Values might sound like a soft exercise, but they're not. They're decision-making tools in disguise. When you're not sure whether to accept a particular donation, your values guide you. When you're torn between two program approaches, your values break the tie. When you're hiring, your values tell you what kind of person belongs on your team.

Lisa picked five. Accessibility—services available to all families regardless of income, insurance, or background. Dignity—every family treated with respect, no judgment, no stigma. Accountability—transparent about resources, honest about results. Collaboration—working with other providers, not competing against them. Persistence—never giving up on a family just because the system makes it hard.

Those aren't wall decorations. They're operational guidelines. When Lisa's organization eventually faces a tough call about whether to serve a family outside their usual area, accessibility guides the decision. When they're choosing between a flashy marketing campaign and investing in direct services, accountability helps them prioritize. When a case hits a dead end and the system keeps putting up walls, persistence reminds them why they exist.

Pick three to five values for your organization. For each one, write a brief note on what it looks like in practice—not just the word itself, but how it actually shows up in daily work. Values without practical meaning are just slogans. Values with clear definitions are tools you'll use every week.

The Regular Person Guide

PUTTING IT ALL TOGETHER

If you've worked through every exercise in this chapter, you've got something powerful in front of you: a clear problem statement, a detailed picture of the people you serve, a concrete solution, a mission, a vision, and a set of values. That's the foundation of your organization. Everything you build from here—programs, board, fundraising, legal documents—rests on this.

Here's Lisa's foundation, assembled all in one place. Problem: families in Franklin County face months-long waits for children's mental health services, and parents lack the knowledge to navigate the system. People: low to moderate income families with children ages five to eighteen experiencing mental health challenges. Solution: navigation program connecting families with providers, paperwork help, follow-up, plus community workshops. Mission: "The Family Bridge Project connects Franklin County families with affordable mental health services for their children by providing personalized navigation support, so that no family has to face the mental health system alone." Vision: "A community where every family can access the mental health support their children need, when they need it, without barriers." Values: accessibility, dignity, accountability, collaboration, persistence.

That's clear, focused, and specific. Anyone reading it gets the picture immediately. That clarity isn't an accident—it's the result of the deliberate work Lisa put in this chapter. Yours should feel just as sharp.

BEFORE YOU MOVE ON

One more thing before we keep going. Don't rush through this work to get to the "exciting" parts of starting a nonprofit. I know the legal stuff and fundraising might feel more tangible, more real. But the foundation you built here is what makes all of that meaningful. An organization without a clear mission is just a collection of activities. An organization with a clear mission is a force.

Share what you've written with people you trust. Ask them to explain it back to you in their own words. If they can, you nailed it. If they look confused or start asking a bunch of clarifying questions, go back and refine. This isn't a document you write once and stick in a drawer. It's a living thing that should be clear enough for anyone and compelling enough to make them want in.

In Chapter 4, we're going to tackle something that might seem obvious but turns out to be trickier than you'd think: figuring out exactly who your audience is. And I'm not just talking about the people you serve—I'm talking about the supporters, funders, volunteers, and champions who'll make your work possible. You'll learn five practical research methods you can use without spending a dime, and I'll introduce you to Denise, whose community research completely changed the direction of her nonprofit—for the better. The work you did in this chapter is going to be your foundation for all of it.

You've done the hard thinking. Now let's start building.

CHAPTER 4: CHOOSING YOUR AUDIENCE

"You can't serve people you don't understand."

Last chapter, you built the foundation—mission, vision, values. You identified the problem and described the people you want to help. Now we need to go deeper. Because knowing you want to help "low-income families" or "at-risk youth" is a start, but it's not enough. To build a nonprofit that actually works, you need to understand your audience with a level of detail that most founders never bother to develop.

And here's the thing that catches people off guard: you don't have just one audience. You've got two. The first is the people you serve—the individuals and families who'll benefit directly from your programs. The second is the community of supporters who'll fund your work, volunteer their time, spread the word, and champion your cause. These two groups are equally important, and they're not the same people. You need to understand both.

This chapter is also about research—but not the kind that requires a graduate degree or a fancy database. The kind anyone can do with a phone, a notebook, and a willingness to listen. By the end, you'll know your audiences inside and out, and you'll have real information, not just assumptions, guiding your decisions.

UNDERSTANDING YOUR TWO AUDIENCES

Quick example to make this concrete. Say you're starting a nonprofit that provides free after-school music lessons for kids in underserved neighborhoods. Audience one—the people you serve—are the kids and their families. You need to understand their lives. Do the parents work multiple jobs? Is transportation a problem? What time do kids get out of school? What would make a parent feel safe sending their child to your program?

Audience two—your supporters—looks completely different. Local business owners who might sponsor instruments. Music teachers who'd volunteer. Parents from wealthier neighborhoods who value music education and want to help extend that chance to other kids. Foundations that fund arts programming. Community leaders who can open doors.

These folks aren't participating in your after-school program, but without them, the program doesn't exist.

The mistake a lot of new founders make is obsessing over one audience and forgetting the other. Some get so locked in on the people they want to serve that they never think about who's going to pay for it all. Others get so caught up in impressing funders that they lose touch with the community they're supposed to be helping. You need both. The research in this chapter makes sure you understand both.

GETTING TO KNOW THE PEOPLE YOU SERVE

There's no substitute for talking directly to the people you want to help. None. You can read all the reports and statistics you want, but until you sit down with real people and hear their stories in their own words, you're building on assumptions. And assumptions are a terrible foundation for anything.

When I say "talk to people," I don't mean formal surveys or clinical interviews. I mean genuine conversations. Coffee. Community events. Listening at church, at school pickup, at the laundromat. The best nonprofit research doesn't feel like research at all. It feels like a neighbor who cares enough to ask, "What's going on in your life, and how can things get better?"

HOW LISA DID IT

Lisa organized informal listening sessions. She put up flyers at the library, the community center, and two elementary schools: "Struggling to find mental health support for your child? A group of parents is meeting to share experiences and talk about solutions. Coffee and snacks provided."

Eleven people showed up to the first one. Lisa didn't come with a presentation or an agenda. She came with a few open questions: What's your experience been like trying to find services? What was the hardest part? What would've made it easier? If a program existed to help you navigate all this, what would you want it to look like?

What she heard changed the way she thought about everything. She'd assumed the biggest barrier was a shortage of providers. That was part of it, sure. But what she kept hearing, over and over, was that parents didn't even know where to start. They didn't know what a referral was or how to get one. They didn't understand their insurance. They were embarrassed to ask for help because of the stigma. Several described calling one office, getting told to call another, sitting on hold, being handed forms they didn't understand, and eventually just giving up.

One mother said something that became a guiding principle for Lisa's entire organization: "It's not just that there aren't enough therapists. It's that the whole system is designed for people who already know how it works. If you don't know the language and you don't know the steps, you're invisible." That sentence hit Lisa like a freight train. She wasn't just going to connect families with services. She was going to walk beside them through a system that wasn't built for them.

She also picked up practical details that shaped her program design. Most parents couldn't make daytime appointments. Transportation was a huge barrier. Some families weren't comfortable with therapy for cultural or religious reasons but were open to other kinds of support. Each insight influenced how Lisa set her hours, structured her services, and trained her navigators.

FIVE SIMPLE RESEARCH METHODS ANYONE CAN USE

You don't need a research budget or a team of analysts. Here are five methods you can start using today.

LISTENING SESSIONS AND COMMUNITY CONVERSATIONS

This is what Lisa did, and it's the single most valuable tool in your kit. Gather a small group of people affected by the problem. Create a comfortable space. Ask open-ended questions and listen way more than you talk. Take notes but don't make it feel like an interrogation. Aim for at least three or four sessions with different groups so you're hearing a range of voices, not just the loudest ones.

ONE-ON-ONE CONVERSATIONS WITH PEOPLE IN THE FIELD

Talk to folks who are already working on your issue—social workers, teachers, healthcare providers, faith leaders, government employees. These people have front-line knowledge you'll never get from a website. They know where the gaps are. They know what's been tried before and what flopped. They can also become allies and referral sources down the road.

When Lisa reached out to school counselors, she learned most of them had lists of families needing mental health referrals but zero time to follow up. One counselor told her: "I can identify the kids who need help. What I can't do is hold every parent's hand through the process. If your organization can do that, you'll fill a gap I see every single day." That conversation confirmed Lisa's concept and gave her a referral partner before she'd even launched.

REVIEWING WHAT ALREADY EXISTS

Before you build something new, take a hard look at what's already out there. Search online for organizations working on similar issues. Check your local United Way's directory. Look at county and city government websites for publicly funded programs. Call 211—it's a free helpline in most areas that connects people with local services. You're not just trying to avoid duplication. You're trying to understand the landscape you're stepping into.

You might discover five organizations tackling your issue but none serving a particular neighborhood. You might learn that an organization closed last year, leaving a gap you could fill. You might find a program in another city that's cracked the same problem and that you could adapt. All of it makes you smarter and more prepared.

USING FREE DATA AND PUBLIC REPORTS

A huge amount of useful information is sitting out there for free. The U.S. Census Bureau has detailed demographics for every community in the country. Your state health department publishes reports on public health issues. The County Health Rankings website compares outcomes across communities. School districts publish data on attendance, performance, and behavior. The Substance Abuse and Mental Health Services Administration tracks mental health trends by state and county.

Data won't give you the personal stories, but it'll help you understand the scope of what you're dealing with. When Lisa found that her county had one-third the child psychiatrists per capita compared to the state average, that number became a centerpiece of her grant applications and community presentations. Numbers plus stories—that's a compelling case.

SIMPLY PAYING ATTENTION

Some of the best research is just keeping your eyes and ears open. Attend community meetings. Read the local paper. Follow neighborhood social media groups. Pay attention to what people are talking about, complaining about, asking for. Sometimes the most important insight doesn't come from a formal method at all—it comes from a comment someone drops in a Facebook group or a conversation you overhear at the store. Stay curious and stay connected.

GETTING TO KNOW YOUR SUPPORTERS

Now let's talk about your second audience: the people who'll fund, volunteer for, and champion your organization. Understanding them takes a different kind of homework.

Start by thinking about who's likely to care about your cause. For Lisa, that list included parents with resources who'd been through similar struggles, local businesses that valued community health, healthcare organizations that would benefit from a referral partner, mental health professionals passionate about access, foundations and government agencies funding behavioral health, and faith communities focused on family well-being.

Each of these groups has different reasons for showing up. A parent who's been through the same struggle might give because they want to spare other families the pain. A local business might sponsor an event for the community visibility. A foundation might fund you because your data demonstrates a clear gap. Understanding what drives each group is how you build relationships that last.

Lisa started cultivating supporters early, well before she had official nonprofit status. She showed up at chamber of commerce meetings. She called the community foundation to learn about funding opportunities. She connected with a Rotary Club that had a health committee. She wasn't asking for money yet—she was building relationships, learning what mattered to potential supporters, and planting seeds that would grow when the time was right.

WHAT IF YOUR RESEARCH TELLS YOU SOMETHING UNEXPECTED?

This takes guts to face: your research might tell you something you didn't want to hear. Maybe someone's already doing what you planned, and doing it well. Maybe the problem isn't what you thought. Maybe the people you want to serve flat-out tell you they need something different.

That's what happened to Denise. She wanted to start a nonprofit providing free clothing to families in need. She had the idea, the passion, and a spare bedroom stuffed with donated clothes. But when she started talking to families, she heard something she wasn't expecting. "We can get clothes," one mother told her. "What we can't get is help paying our utility bills in winter. My kids have coats, but our heat got cut off last February."

Other families said the same thing in different ways. Clothing wasn't their most pressing need. Energy assistance was. Denise had a choice: ignore what she heard and push ahead with her original plan, or let the community's actual needs steer her direction. She chose to listen. She pivoted to emergency utility assistance and winter clothing distribution. Her organization became more relevant, more impactful, and better supported—because she built it around what people actually needed, not what she'd assumed they needed.

Your research might also reveal that the best move isn't starting something new at all, but helping existing organizations coordinate. Maybe your community has a food bank, a housing nonprofit, and a job training program, but none of them talk to each other. Families fall through the cracks because nobody's connecting the dots. In that case, your highest-impact play might be building a coalition rather than adding another standalone to an already fragmented landscape.

None of this is failure. It's wisdom. The goal isn't to start a nonprofit for the sake of having one. The goal is to make a difference. If research points you somewhere you didn't expect, follow it. Your community will thank you.

HOW THIS RESEARCH MAKES YOU CREDIBLE FROM DAY ONE

Here's something first-time founders don't always realize: the research you do in this chapter isn't just for your own benefit. It's one of the most powerful credibility builders you've got. When you sit across from a potential funder and say, "I held four listening sessions with families in our target area, and here's what they told us"—that funder knows you're serious. When you can cite local data, name the other organizations in your space, and describe the needs of your community based on actual conversations? That's what separates organizations that get funded from the ones that don't.

Lisa kept notes from every conversation, every session, every stakeholder meeting. She pulled it all together into a simple document she called her "community needs summary"—just a few pages with key findings, quotes from families, relevant stats, and a list of organizations she'd connected with. Nothing fancy. But that document became one of her most valuable tools. She referenced it in grant applications, board recruitment conversations, and community presentations. It showed that her organization wasn't built on one person's assumptions. It was built on the voices of the community itself.

YOUR ASSIGNMENT BEFORE MOVING ON

Before you flip to the next chapter, do three things. First, hold at least one listening session or have at least five one-on-one conversations with people directly affected by the problem you want to tackle. Ask open questions. Write down what you hear. Second, reach out to at least three people already working in your space—a social worker, a teacher, a nonprofit director, whoever makes sense—and ask them about the gaps they see. Third, spend an hour or two online digging into data and existing programs related to your issue in your community.

This isn't busywork. These are the building blocks of a credible, community-driven organization. The insights you gather now will shape your programs, strengthen your fundraising, and earn you trust on both sides—from the people you serve and the people who make your work possible.

In Chapter 5, we're getting into one of the most important and most misunderstood parts of starting a nonprofit: building your board of directors. You'll learn what a board actually does (and doesn't do), how many people you need, what qualities to look for, and how to ask someone to serve without making it weird. We'll also have an honest conversation about the founder-board relationship—because that dynamic can either be your greatest asset or your biggest headache, and it's all about how you set it up from the start.

The research you've done in these first four chapters means you're not walking into board recruitment empty-handed. You've got a clear mission, a defined audience, and real community knowledge behind you. That's exactly where you want to be.

The Regular Person Guide
CHAPTER 5: PUTTING TOGETHER THE BOARD

"Your board doesn't need to be perfect. It needs to be present."

If there's one topic that makes new founders break into a cold sweat, it's the board of directors. The idea of recruiting a group of people to oversee your organization—this thing that barely exists yet—can feel overwhelming. Who'd want to serve on the board of something that's still basically an idea and a napkin? Where do you find these people? What do you even say to them? And what happens when a group of people suddenly has legal authority over the thing you created?

Take a breath. Building a board isn't as scary as it sounds. Done right, your board becomes one of your greatest assets—people who believe in your mission, bring skills you don't have, share the weight of hard decisions, and keep your organization honest. Done poorly, a board can be a source of endless frustration and dysfunction. This chapter is about making sure you land on the right side of that line.

WHAT DOES A BOARD OF DIRECTORS ACTUALLY DO?

First, let's clear up the biggest misunderstanding out there. The board doesn't run the day-to-day operations of your organization. That's your job. The board's role is governance, not management. Getting those two things confused causes more problems in new nonprofits than almost anything else.

Governance means the board handles the big picture. They set the organization's overall direction. They make sure you're fulfilling the mission. They approve the budget and keep an eye on whether money's being handled responsibly. They hire and evaluate the executive director. They make sure you're following the law. And they lend their credibility, connections, and expertise to help things succeed.

Here's a way to think about it. If your nonprofit were a ship, you'd be the captain—steering day to day, managing the crew, making course corrections in real time. The board would be the ship's owners. They decide where the ship is headed, make sure it's seaworthy, review the captain's performance, and provide resources for the voyage. What they don't do is stand on deck telling the crew which ropes to pull. They trust the captain for that.

In practice, your board will meet regularly—monthly, bimonthly, or quarterly depending on your needs—to review finances, talk strategy, approve major decisions, and offer guidance. Between meetings, individual members might help with fundraising, make introductions, or advise you on specific problems. But they're not in the office every day, and they shouldn't be hovering over your programs.

WHO SHOULD BE ON YOUR FOUNDING BOARD?

Good news: your founding board doesn't need to be a dream team of wealthy executives and power brokers. What it needs is a small group of people who genuinely care about your mission, are willing to do real work, and bring some kind of value—even if that value is simply showing up consistently and asking good questions.

That said, certain qualities matter more than others.

BELIEF IN THE MISSION

Non-negotiable. Every person on your board has to genuinely care about the problem you're solving. Someone who joined because it'd look good on a resume or because they owed a friend a favor will drain your energy and contribute nothing. Look for people whose eyes light up when you describe what you're building—people with a personal connection to the issue through their own experience, their work, or their community involvement.

WILLINGNESS TO ACTUALLY WORK

Board membership isn't an honorary title. It takes time, attention, and follow-through. You need people who'll show up to meetings, read the materials beforehand, engage in discussions, and do what they say they'll do. Make this clear before anyone commits. A board of five people who actually show up is infinitely better than fifteen who don't.

DIFFERENT SKILLS AND PERSPECTIVES

You don't want a board where everybody thinks the same way. Aim for a mix: someone with financial chops—an accountant, a bookkeeper, a business owner who manages budgets. Someone who understands your issue area. Someone with community connections who can open doors. And someone who represents the people you serve—a person who's lived the experience your organization addresses and can keep the work grounded in reality.

Lisa built her board with intention. Her retired-accountant neighbor. A school counselor who knew the mental health landscape. A local pastor whose church served many of the families Lisa wanted to reach. A mother who'd navigated the system for her own child. And a small business owner active in the chamber of commerce. Five people, five different lenses, every one of them deeply invested in the mission.

HOW BIG SHOULD YOUR BOARD BE?

Most states require at least three members to incorporate. Some require more—check your state before you finalize. Beyond the legal minimum, the question is what actually works for a startup.

I recommend five to seven. Three is technically legal most places, but it gives you almost no room for diverse perspectives and makes it hard to share the load. Twelve or fifteen is way too many—you'll spend more energy herding cats than making progress. Five to seven is the sweet spot: big enough for range, small enough to make decisions efficiently, manageable enough to build real relationships with each member. You can always expand later.

TERMS, OFFICERS, AND STRUCTURE

Your bylaws—which we'll tackle in the next chapter—will spell out term lengths and officer positions. But it helps to know the basics now so you can have informed conversations with recruits.

Board terms are typically two or three years. Many organizations let members serve two consecutive terms before rotating off for a year. Stagger your terms from the start. If everyone's term expires at the same time, you could lose your entire board in one shot. Staggering keeps continuity intact.

Every board needs officers. At minimum: a Chair or President who leads meetings and connects board to executive director. A Secretary who takes minutes and keeps records. A Treasurer who oversees finances and reporting. Some add a Vice Chair as backup. These roles get filled by your board members and are elected by the board itself.

THE FOUNDER AND THE BOARD: A RELATIONSHIP THAT REQUIRES HONESTY

This is the section a lot of nonprofit books skip, and it's the one that causes the most pain when it goes wrong. So let's be direct.

As the founder, you don't own this organization. Even though it was your idea, your sweat, and your sleepless nights that brought it to life—the nonprofit belongs to the public. The board has legal authority to make major decisions, including decisions about your role. That's not a threat. It's how nonprofits are structured, and understanding it from day one saves you a world of grief later.

In practice, most founding boards are deeply supportive and give the founder plenty of room to lead. But the legal reality is clear: the board governs, the executive director reports to the board. Ignoring that dynamic or trying to control the board leads to dysfunction—and in worst cases, founders getting pushed out of the organizations they created.

The healthiest approach is mutual respect, transparency, and straight talk. Share information openly. Welcome tough questions. Don't treat the board as a rubber stamp. At the same time, the board should respect your expertise, trust your judgment on daily operations, and resist the temptation to micromanage.

Lisa nailed this from the start. When she recruited her board, she was upfront: "I started this thing, and I'm deeply invested in it. But I need people who'll ask hard questions and push back when I'm wrong. I don't want a board that just nods along. I want a board that makes this organization better than I could make it by myself." That honesty set the right tone from day one.

HOW TO ASK SOMEONE TO SERVE

Recruiting starts with a conversation, not a formal letter. Meet someone for coffee. Have an honest talk about what you're building and why you think they'd be a great fit.

Here's a loose framework. Lead with your story—why this matters to you personally. Describe the mission and the problem. Explain the board's role and what you'd expect—how often you'd meet, the time commitment, what skills or connections you're hoping they'd bring. Be straight about where things stand. Haven't incorporated yet? Say so. Zero dollars in the bank? Say that too. People respect honesty way more than a polished pitch.

Then just ask: "Would you be interested in serving on our founding board?" Give them time. Don't pressure anyone into a yes on the spot. And be ready for some nos—that's not a rejection of you. It usually means the timing's off. Thank them and ask if they'd support the organization another way—volunteering, donating, making introductions.

Lisa approached ten people over three weeks. Seven showed interest. After follow-up conversations about expectations, five committed. The two who said no offered to help with events. Both became active supporters down the line. Lisa was glad she didn't take it personally.

THE LEGAL RESPONSIBILITIES OF BOARD MEMBERS

Before anyone signs on, they need to understand the legal duties. This isn't about scaring people—it's about making sure everybody goes in with open eyes. There are three duties.

Duty of care. Stay informed. Attend meetings. Read the financials. Ask questions. Use good judgment. In plain English: pay attention and take it seriously.

Duty of loyalty. Put the organization's interests ahead of your own. Don't use your position to benefit yourself, your family, or your business. If there's a conflict of interest—say the board's considering hiring a company you own—disclose it and step out of the vote.

Duty of obedience. Make sure the organization follows its mission and complies with all laws, regulations, and its own governing documents. No randomly changing the mission, no ignoring legal requirements.

Lisa kept it simple: "Being on this board means you pay attention, you act in the organization's best interest, and you help us follow the rules. Do those three things and you're doing your job." Nobody ran for the door. Several said they appreciated the transparency.

THE BOARD DO'S AND DON'TS

A practical reference you can share with your board and come back to as the organization grows.

DO'S

- Show up to meetings. Consistently. If you can't make one, let the chair know ahead of time and read the minutes after.
- Come prepared. Read the agenda, financials, and materials before the meeting. Don't be the person catching up while everyone else is ready to decide.
- Ask questions. If something doesn't make sense—a budget line, a program decision, a policy—speak up. Good questions protect the organization.
- Support fundraising. Every member should contribute something financially, even modestly, and help raise funds however they can—introductions, events, thank-you notes, sharing the story.
- Respect the line between governance and management. Set direction, approve budgets, evaluate leadership, ensure accountability. Then let staff do their jobs.
- Disclose conflicts of interest immediately. If you've got a stake in something the board is deciding, say so before the discussion starts.
- Be an ambassador. Talk positively about the mission in your community. Be proud of what you're building together.

DON'TS

- Don't treat meetings as optional. Chronic no-shows undermine the entire board.
- Don't use your position for personal gain. No steering contracts to your business, hiring relatives, or tapping organizational resources for yourself.
- Don't micromanage staff. Got concerns? Raise them with the executive director—don't go around them.
- Don't make commitments on the organization's behalf without board approval. No solo contract-signing or financial promises.

- Don't air internal disagreements publicly. Board conflict stays in the boardroom. Period.
- Don't stay if you've lost the fire. Better to step down and make room than to occupy a seat while contributing nothing.
- Don't rubber-stamp budgets or ignore financials. If you don't understand something, ask. Don't just nod along.
- Don't let anyone—including the founder—operate without accountability. Your job is oversight, even when you love and trust the leader.

BUILDING SOMETHING BIGGER THAN YOURSELF

Putting together a board is one of the most important things you'll do as a founder. It's the moment your nonprofit stops being just your idea and becomes a shared endeavor. That can feel vulnerable—you're inviting people into something deeply personal and handing them real authority over its future. But that vulnerability is what gives the organization strength. A nonprofit that depends on one person is fragile. A nonprofit governed by a committed board is resilient.

Lisa's founding board wasn't a group of all-stars. It was five ordinary people who cared about families in their community and were willing to roll up their sleeves. They didn't always agree—and that was a feature, not a bug. Different perspectives made the organization stronger. Shared commitment kept them united when decisions got tough.

In Chapter 6, we're diving into the legal paperwork that officially brings your nonprofit to life—articles of incorporation, bylaws, and all the documents the state and federal government want to see. I'll walk you through what each document is, what needs to be in it, what language the IRS is looking for, and the common mistakes that trip people up or get applications kicked back. Your board plays a key role in this process, so make sure your people are in place before you move forward.

You don't need a perfect board. You need a present one. Find your people, have honest conversations, set clear expectations, and start building something together that none of you could build alone.

CHAPTER 6: THE INCORPORATION PAPERWORK

"Yes, it's paperwork. But it's paperwork you can absolutely handle."

Alright, it's time to make this thing official. Everything you've done so far—developing the idea, defining the mission, researching your community, building your board—has been preparation. Important preparation, but preparation all the same. This chapter is where your nonprofit starts to exist in the eyes of the law.

I know "paperwork" makes some people want to close the book and take a nap. I get it. Legal documents aren't exciting. But here's the thing: they're not as complicated as they look, and you don't need a law degree to handle them. Having an attorney review your documents is smart if you can swing it, but it's not required. What you need is a clear explanation of what each document does and what goes in it. That's what this chapter delivers.

We're focusing on two key documents: your articles of incorporation, which officially create your organization as a legal entity in your state, and your bylaws, which are the internal rules governing how your organization operates. Think of the articles as your organization's birth certificate and the bylaws as your household rules. Both are essential. Both are more straightforward than you'd think.

WHAT IS INCORPORATION AND WHY DOES IT MATTER?

Incorporation is the legal process of turning your nonprofit from an idea shared by a group of people into a formal entity under state law. Before you incorporate, you're just a group with a plan. After, you're a legal entity that can open bank accounts, sign contracts, apply for grants, and—this is the big one—protect its founders and board members from personal liability.

That liability piece deserves emphasis. When you incorporate, you create a legal wall between the organization and the individuals running it. If the nonprofit gets sued or takes on debt, the personal assets of board members and founders are generally protected. Without incorporation, if something goes wrong—a lawsuit, an unpaid bill, an accident at an event—the people involved could be on the hook personally.

Every state has its own process, but the general flow is the same: prepare your articles of incorporation, file them with the Secretary of State's office, pay a filing fee, and wait for approval. Fees range from around twenty-five bucks in some states to several hundred in others. Most states let you file online.

Lisa filed hers on a Tuesday evening after work. Kitchen table, laptop, cup of coffee, and the notes she'd been building through this whole process. From pulling up the state's online system to hitting "submit" took about two hours. Filing fee: ninety-nine dollars. Two weeks later, she had her approval. The Family Bridge Project was officially real.

ARTICLES OF INCORPORATION: WHAT GOES IN THEM

Your articles formally establish your nonprofit corporation under state law. They get filed with your state government and become public record. Most are just a few pages, but the language matters—especially since the IRS will review them closely when you apply for tax-exempt status.

THE NAME

Your official legal name. Before you settle on one, search your state's Secretary of State database to make sure nobody else has it. Most states have a free online search tool. Many states require a corporate designator like "Inc." or "Incorporated."

Lisa chose "The Family Bridge Project, Inc." She searched the database, confirmed it was available, and reserved it before filing. Small step, but important—you don't want to fill out everything only to discover someone beat you to the name.

THE PURPOSE STATEMENT

This describes why your organization exists, and it needs specific language to satisfy the IRS. They want to see that you're organized exclusively for exempt purposes under Section 501(c)(3).

Include both a general and a specific statement. General: "This corporation is organized exclusively for charitable and educational purposes within the meaning of Section 501(c)(3) of the Internal Revenue Code." Specific: "Specifically, the corporation will connect families in Franklin County with affordable mental health services for their children through navigation support, community education, and advocacy."

Don't skip the IRS language. It's not optional. If your articles don't include it, your tax-exempt application will get delayed or denied.

THE REGISTERED AGENT

Every corporation needs a registered agent—a person or company designated to receive official legal documents on the organization's behalf. Must have a physical address in the state. Many founders serve as their own agent initially. You can also hire a service for fifty to a few hundred dollars a year if you'd rather keep your home address off public filings.

THE INCORPORATOR

The person who signs and files the articles. Usually the founder. The incorporator's role ends once the articles are approved—after that, the board takes over.

THE DISSOLUTION CLAUSE

Describes what happens to assets if the organization ever shuts down. The IRS requires language stating that remaining assets go to another 501(c)(3) or a government entity—not to founders, board members, or anyone personally. It feels odd to write about closing when you're just getting started, but the IRS and most states require it.

THE PROHIBITION ON PRIVATE BENEFIT

Your articles need language saying no part of the organization's earnings will benefit any private individual. You're absolutely allowed to pay people for their work—salaries, consulting fees, all fair game—as long as compensation is reasonable. What you can't do is funnel the nonprofit's money to individuals as if it were a for-profit business.

BYLAWS: YOUR ORGANIZATION'S INTERNAL RULEBOOK

If the articles are your birth certificate, the bylaws are your household rules. They're not filed with the state, but they're legally binding. They govern how the board operates, how decisions get made, and how internal affairs are handled. Good bylaws prevent confusion, reduce conflict, and make sure everyone knows how things work.

BOARD OF DIRECTORS

How many members, how they're selected, term lengths, how vacancies get filled, and how a member can be removed. Lisa's bylaws: five to nine directors, three-year terms, two consecutive terms max, new directors by majority vote, removal by two-thirds vote for missing three consecutive meetings or harmful conduct.

OFFICERS

Describes the positions—Chair, Vice Chair, Secretary, Treasurer—and their responsibilities. Covers election, term length, and removal.

MEETINGS

One of the most important sections. How often the board meets, whether remote participation counts, advance notice requirements, and what constitutes a quorum—the minimum number needed for official business. Quorum is typically a simple majority. Five board members means three must be present to vote. Without quorum, you can talk but you can't decide.

Lisa's bylaws: at least four meetings per year, seven days' notice, phone and video allowed, special meetings as needed.

VOTING PROCEDURES

Most decisions are simple majority—more than half of directors present where quorum exists. Major decisions like amending bylaws, removing a member, or dissolving the organization usually need two-thirds. Spell out which decisions require which threshold so there's never confusion at vote time.

Some bylaws allow action without a meeting through email consent. Useful for urgent items, but use it sparingly. Big stuff deserves real discussion.

COMMITTEES

As you grow, the board may form committees for finance, fundraising, programs. Your bylaws should allow this and make one thing crystal clear: committees recommend, the full board decides.

CONFLICT OF INTEREST POLICY

Sometimes within the bylaws, sometimes separate. Either way, you need one. It requires board members to disclose interests that could influence decisions, describes what counts as a conflict, and spells out what happens—typically, the conflicted member steps out. The IRS looks for this specifically in your tax-exempt application.

AMENDMENTS

How the bylaws themselves get changed. Typical process: proposed changes distributed in advance, approved by two-thirds vote. Prevents changes on a whim but allows updates as the organization evolves.

WHY GOOD BYLAWS PREVENT DISASTERS

Quick cautionary tale. I worked with an organization whose founders treated bylaws as an afterthought—copied a template off the internet, changed the name, never read it. First year, fine. Then a disagreement blew up between the founder and two board members about a major program. Nobody knew how to resolve it. No voting threshold for big decisions. No dispute process. The conflict escalated, two members quit, and the organization nearly collapsed.

Good bylaws would've prevented all of it. A clear threshold turns a power struggle into a vote. A defined process gives everyone ground rules. Instead, they were flying blind.

Take your bylaws seriously. Read every section. Make sure your board understands them. Don't copy a template blindly—customize it for your organization's needs, size, and culture. Bylaws aren't just legal paperwork. They're the operating manual that keeps things running when the road gets rough.

YOU CAN HANDLE THIS

Lisa completed her articles in one evening. She drafted bylaws over a weekend using a template from her state's nonprofit association as a starting point, then customized based on what she'd learned. The retired accountant on her board reviewed the financial sections. The school counselor looked at meetings and voting. A friend-of-a-friend attorney did a quick review for two hundred dollars. Lisa walked away confident.

You can do this too. The articles and bylaws aren't walls—they're doors. Walk through them and your organization becomes a real legal entity with structure and a framework for decision-making. Not glamorous, but it's the bridge between your idea and your impact.

In Chapter 7, we're tackling the big one: applying for federal tax-exempt status with the IRS. That's the step that gives your organization its 501(c)(3) designation and unlocks tax-deductible donations and grant eligibility. I'll walk you through both IRS forms, break down the application section by section, show you what a strong narrative looks like versus a weak one, and flag the five mistakes that get applications rejected or stuck in limbo. The articles and bylaws you've created here will be part of that application, so take the time to get them right.

Now go file that paperwork. Your nonprofit is waiting to be born.

The Regular Person Guide
CHAPTER 7: COMPLETING YOUR 501(C)(3) APPLICATION

"The IRS isn't trying to trick you. They just want to know you're for real."

If starting a nonprofit has a final boss, this is it. The IRS application for tax-exempt status is the step most founders dread more than anything else. It feels like a high-stakes exam where you're not sure you studied the right material. People worry about saying the wrong thing, checking the wrong box, or getting flagged for an audit before they've served a single person.

Let me put your mind at ease. The application isn't a trap. It's not designed to catch you in a mistake. It's a straightforward process where the IRS asks you to demonstrate that your organization is genuinely set up for a charitable, educational, or other exempt purpose. If you've done the work in the previous chapters—defined your mission, built your board, filed your articles, drafted your bylaws—you've already got most of what you need.

This chapter walks you through the application step by step, in plain English. Which form to use, what each section asks for, how to describe your programs so the IRS gets it, how to build financial projections, and how to avoid the mistakes that cause delays.

WHICH FORM: 1023 OR 1023-EZ?

The IRS gives you two options. Form 1023 is the full, comprehensive application. Form 1023-EZ is the shorter version, created in 2014 for smaller organizations.

The 1023-EZ is available if you project annual gross receipts under $250,000 for the next three years and total assets under $250,000. It's filed online at Pay.gov, costs $275, and most people can knock it out in an hour or two. Processing usually takes a few weeks to a couple months.

Form 1023 is the full deal. Required if you exceed those thresholds or have a more complex structure. Filing fee is $600. It's considerably more detailed—narrative descriptions of your activities, financial projections, supporting documents. Processing runs three to six months, sometimes longer.

So which should you pick? If you qualify for the EZ, it's tempting to take the easier path. For small, straightforward organizations, it's perfectly fine. But I'll be honest with you: the 1023-EZ is so streamlined that it doesn't push you to think deeply about your programs or finances. Some nonprofit experts worry that the ease of approval has led to organizations launching before they were truly ready.

My take: even if you qualify for the EZ, consider whether the discipline of the full form would strengthen your foundation. But if you're small, clear on your mission, and tight on cash, the 1023-EZ is a valid choice.

Lisa qualified for the EZ but filed the full form on a mentor's advice: "Going through the long form is like getting a physical before a marathon. Takes more time, but it makes sure everything's in order." She was glad she listened. The process sharpened her program descriptions and financial plans in ways that served her for years.

WHAT THE IRS IS REALLY LOOKING FOR

Before we dig into the sections, here's the big picture. The IRS is trying to answer a handful of questions. Is this organization genuinely set up for an exempt purpose? Will it actually serve the public good? Is there any sign it's really a front for private benefit or political activity? Does it have adequate governance and financial oversight?

That's it. They're not looking for perfection. They don't expect you to have everything figured out on day one. They want evidence that you're legitimate, thoughtful, and playing by the rules. Show them that, and your application gets approved.

WALKING THROUGH FORM 1023

IDENTIFICATION OF APPLICANT

Basic info: legal name, address, EIN, date of incorporation, contact person. Your EIN—Employer Identification Number—is like a Social Security number for your organization. If you don't have one, apply free on the IRS website. Takes ten minutes. Get this done before you start the 1023.

ORGANIZATIONAL STRUCTURE

Attach your articles of incorporation and bylaws. If you followed Chapter 6, they already contain the language the IRS needs—exempt purpose clause, dissolution clause, prohibition on private benefit. Double-check before you submit. Missing language means the application gets sent back, and that adds months.

NARRATIVE DESCRIPTION OF ACTIVITIES

This is the heart of the application, and it's where most people get tripped up. The IRS wants you to describe all your activities—past, present, and planned—in detail. What you do, how you do it, who benefits, and how it advances your exempt purpose.

The key: write like you're explaining your organization to a smart person who knows nothing about your field. No jargon. No assumptions that the reviewer understands your issue area. Describe your programs step by step, as concretely as possible. Remember the solution you laid out in Chapter 3? That level of specificity is exactly what belongs here.

Here's what Lisa wrote: "The Family Bridge Project operates a family mental health navigation program serving Franklin County, Ohio. When a family contacts our organization, a trained navigator conducts an intake assessment to understand the family's needs, including the child's symptoms, insurance status, and previous attempts to access services. The navigator identifies appropriate providers who accept the family's insurance or offer sliding-scale fees, assists with referral paperwork, schedules appointments, and arranges transportation if needed. Within two weeks, the navigator follows up to confirm the appointment was kept and services are underway. If barriers arose, the navigator works with the family to resolve them."

She continued with her workshops, resource directory, and other activities—all described with the same concrete detail. Notice what she didn't do: she didn't write vague statements about "empowering families" or "raising awareness." She explained exactly what happens when someone interacts with her organization. That's what the IRS needs.

COMPENSATION AND FINANCIAL ARRANGEMENTS

Who's getting paid and how much. Officers, directors, employees, contractors—all disclosed. The IRS is checking for signs that the money's enriching insiders rather than serving the public. For a new org, it's perfectly normal to show minimal or no compensation. If you do plan to pay people, make sure it's reasonable for the position and your area. Paying yourself triple the market rate is a fast way to get flagged.

FINANCIAL DATA AND PROJECTIONS

Financial history (if any) plus projections for this year and the next two. Most new orgs have no history, so the focus is projections. People freeze here because it feels like guessing—and to some extent, it is. But the IRS knows you're estimating. They're not expecting pinpoint accuracy. They want numbers that are reasonable, consistent with your activities, and show you've thought about how the money works.

Lisa's first year: $45,000 in revenue—$15K individual donations, $20K county mental health grant, $10K community foundation grant. Expenses: $20K part-time navigator salary, $5K supplies and tech, $8K workshops, $5K insurance and professional fees, $7K admin. Years two and three showed modest growth as the organization built its track record.

What mattered: her numbers told a coherent story. Revenue and expenses were in the same ballpark. The spending made sense given the programs she described. Growth was realistic, not wildly optimistic. You don't need a Fortune 500 financial plan. You need to show you've thought about money responsibly.

FIVE COMMON MISTAKES THAT DELAY APPLICATIONS

I've seen the same errors trip people up over and over. Avoiding them will save you months of frustration.

Missing required language in your articles. The IRS requires specific clauses about exempt purpose, dissolution, and private benefit. If your articles don't include them—even if your state didn't require it—the application comes back. You'll have to amend your articles and refile before they'll continue processing.

Vague program descriptions. "We help underserved communities" is not a program description. The IRS needs to know exactly what you do, how, who does it, and who benefits. If the reviewer can't picture your organization's daily activities after reading your narrative, you haven't been specific enough.

Financial projections that don't match your activities. If you describe a program needing three full-time staff but your budget shows $30,000 in revenue, the math doesn't work. Your projections need to be consistent with the scale of what you've described. If there's a gap, explain it—note that volunteers will handle the work until grant funding comes through, for example.

No EIN before applying. You need an Employer Identification Number to file Form 1023. It's quick and free, but some people forget and then have to pause mid-application to go get one.

Incomplete submissions. Missing signatures, forgotten attachments, unsigned forms. Sounds basic, but incomplete applications get returned without review. Before you submit, go through the checklist and make sure everything's there.

SAMPLE NARRATIVES FOR DIFFERENT ORGANIZATION TYPES

To give you a feel for what strong narratives look like across different missions, here are a few examples.

A youth mentoring org: "Our organization recruits, trains, and matches adult volunteer mentors with at-risk youth ages 12–18 in the Metro City School District. Each mentor commits to two hours per week for at least one school year. Matches are based on shared interests and geography. All mentors complete a ten-hour training covering adolescent development, active listening, boundary-setting, and mandatory reporting. Staff conduct monthly check-ins with each match."

A food assistance program: "We operate a mobile food pantry delivering fresh produce and shelf-stable food to three low-income neighborhoods every Saturday morning. Families register on-site and receive a box sufficient to supplement meals for a family of four for approximately one week. We partner with the Regional Food Bank for inventory and recruit 15–20 volunteers weekly. We also distribute information about SNAP benefits, WIC programs, and free meal sites."

An arts education nonprofit: "We provide free after-school visual arts classes for children ages 6–14 at the Eastside Community Center three days per week during the school year. Classes are taught by a certified art teacher and cover drawing, painting, ceramics, and mixed media. Each eight-week session ends with a community show. All materials are free to participants. We also run a July summer arts camp serving up to 40 children per session."

Each of these tells the IRS exactly what the organization does, who it serves, how programs are delivered, and what happens as a result. Use them as models—adapt the structure to fit your activities.

FEES, TIMELINE, AND WHAT TO DO WHILE YOU WAIT

Filing fee for 1023-EZ: $275. For the full 1023: $600. Both paid online at submission. Not refundable, so make sure your application's complete before you file.

Processing times: the EZ usually takes a few weeks to two months. The full 1023 runs three to six months, sometimes longer during busy periods. The IRS sends a confirmation when they receive your application and will reach out if they need more information.

Here's the good news: you're not stuck in limbo while you wait. You can start operating. As long as your articles are filed and you're operating consistently with your exempt purpose, you can begin serving people. Once approved, your 501(c)(3) status is typically retroactive to the date you incorporated—so any donations received during the waiting period count as tax-deductible.

Use the time. Build your community presence. Attend events, network, develop your website, recruit volunteers. Apply for grants that accept applications from organizations with pending status. Draft your first real grant proposal so it's ready to go the minute your determination letter arrives.

Lisa used her wait wisely. She launched a pilot navigation program with volunteers, served a dozen families in the first two months, built relationships with local providers, and drafted her first grant application. By the time the IRS approved her four months later, The Family Bridge Project was already operational, already serving families, and already building a reputation.

YOU'RE CLOSER THAN YOU THINK

The IRS application looks intimidating, and the fees and waiting can feel like barriers. But thousands of people complete it every year, many with no legal or financial background. They succeed because they understand what's being asked, they describe their organizations honestly and specifically, and they submit complete applications.

You've already done the hardest work. Mission defined. Board built. Articles filed. Bylaws drafted. The 501(c)(3) application is just the next step in a process you've been building toward since Chapter 1.

In Chapter 8, we're getting into one of my favorite topics—and probably the most important chapter in this entire book: designing your program. Not just what you'll do, but how you'll know it's actually working. You'll learn about logic models, outcome measurement, and the difference between being busy and being effective. I'll tell you the story of two food pantries—one that stayed stuck for years and one that landed a major grant—and the surprising thing that set them apart.

But first, file that application. Then go celebrate. You've earned it.

CHAPTER 8: CREATING THE PROGRAM

"Good intentions open the door. Good programs change lives."

This is the most important chapter in this book. I'm not saying that to be dramatic. I'm saying it because everything else—the legal paperwork, the fundraising, the board meetings, the tax filings—exists to support one thing: the programs your organization delivers. Programs are the reason your nonprofit exists. They are the vehicle through which your mission becomes real, tangible change in people's lives. If your programs are well designed, well delivered, and regularly evaluated, your organization will thrive. If they're not, nothing else will save you.

Too many new nonprofits jump straight from filing their paperwork to delivering services without ever sitting down to design their programs deliberately. They start doing activities that feel helpful without thinking through whether those activities will actually produce the results they want. The founder shows up with good intentions, works incredibly hard, and six months later can't explain what difference the organization has made. That isn't a failure of effort. It is a failure of design.

This chapter is going to teach you how to design a program from scratch, how to build a simple logic model that connects your activities to your desired outcomes, how to measure whether your program is actually working, and how to use what you learn to improve over time. We are going to take this step by step, in plain English, with examples you can adapt for your own organization. By the end of this chapter, you'll have a framework for creating programs that don't just feel good—they do good, and you can prove it.

WHY PROGRAM DESIGN MATTERS MORE THAN YOU THINK

Let me tell you about two organizations that both set out to reduce hunger in their community. The first organization, which we'll call Hope Pantry, opened its doors and started handing out bags of groceries to anyone who showed up. The founder was a generous, compassionate person who worked tirelessly. Every Saturday, dozens of families lined up, received their groceries, and went home.

Hope Pantry served hundreds of families in its first year. But when a foundation asked the founder what impact the program was having, she couldn't answer. Were families eating better? Were children healthier? Were families moving toward greater food security, or were the same families coming back every single week without their situations improving? The founder had no idea because she had never designed the program to track those things.

The second organization, Community Nourish, also distributed food. But before they opened their doors, they sat down and thought carefully about what they were trying to accomplish. Their goal wasn't just to hand out food but to help families achieve greater food security over time. So in addition to weekly food distribution, they offered monthly cooking classes that taught families how to prepare healthy meals on a tight budget.

They connected families with SNAP benefits enrollment assistance. They partnered with a local community garden where families could grow their own produce. And they tracked every family's progress, measuring not just how many bags of groceries they distributed, but whether families were accessing additional food resources, whether children's school attendance improved, and whether families were reporting less food insecurity over time.

Both organizations were doing good work. Both founders cared deeply. But Community Nourish could demonstrate that their programs were actually changing people's lives, while Hope Pantry could only demonstrate that they were busy. When it came time to apply for a major grant, Community Nourish had the data, the design, and the story to win the funding. Hope Pantry didn't. That is the difference program design makes.

START WITH THE PROBLEM, NOT THE SOLUTION

The most common mistake in program design is starting with an activity and working backward to justify it. Someone decides they want to run an after-school tutoring program, and then they look for a problem that fits. This is backwards. Good program design starts with a deep understanding of the problem and then works forward to identify the activities most likely to solve it.

You already did significant work on this in earlier chapters when you defined your problem statement, identified your target population, and described the specific barriers they face. Now we're going to take that understanding and use it to build a program that directly addresses those barriers.

Let's return to Lisa. Her problem statement, which she developed in Chapter 3, was clear: families in Franklin County face months-long wait times for children's mental health services, and parents lack the knowledge and support to navigate a complex system. When Lisa dug deeper through her community research in Chapter 4, she identified three specific barriers: parents didn't know what services existed, the referral process was confusing and bureaucratic, and stigma prevented many families from seeking help in the first place.

Each of those barriers suggests a different type of program activity. The lack of knowledge suggests the need for information and education. The confusing referral process suggests the need for hands-on navigation support. The stigma barrier suggests the need for community outreach and normalization. Lisa's program wasn't a random collection of activities. It was a deliberate response to documented barriers, with each activity designed to address a specific piece of the puzzle.

LEARNING WHAT ACTUALLY WORKS

Before you finalize your program design, take the time to learn what has already been tried—both what worked and what didn't. You don't need to reinvent the wheel. Other organizations, researchers, and communities have tackled similar problems, and their experiences can save you enormous amounts of time, money, and heartache.

There are several ways to learn what works. First, look at organizations in other communities that address the same issue. What programs do they offer? How are they structured? What results have they achieved? Many nonprofits publish annual reports on their websites that describe their programs and outcomes. You can also call or email program directors at these organizations and ask questions. Most nonprofit leaders are happy to share what they've learned with someone working on a similar mission.

Second, look for published research on your issue area. If you're working on youth mentoring, there's a substantial body of research on what makes mentoring programs effective. If you're working on food insecurity, there's research on which interventions produce lasting change versus short-term relief. You don't need to become a researcher yourself.

A few hours of reading can give you a solid understanding of what the evidence says about effective approaches to your problem.

Third, talk to the professionals who work with your target population every day. Teachers, social workers, healthcare providers, and community leaders have practical knowledge that no report can capture. They know what families actually struggle with, what programs people actually use, and what approaches fall flat despite looking good on paper.

Lisa consulted all three sources. She studied mental health navigation programs in other states and found that the most successful ones paired families with a single, consistent navigator rather than routing them through a call center. She read research showing that follow-up contact within two weeks of a referral dramatically increased the likelihood that families actually connected with services.

And she talked to local school counselors who told her that evening and weekend availability was essential because most parents couldn't take time off work for daytime appointments. Each of these insights shaped her program design in concrete ways.

THE LOGIC MODEL: YOUR PROGRAM'S BLUEPRINT

A logic model is a simple tool that maps out how your program is supposed to work. It connects the dots between what you put into the program, what you do, and what changes as a result. If that sounds complicated, it's not. A logic model is essentially a chain of cause and effect: if we invest these resources, and we do these activities, then these things will happen for the people we serve.

A basic logic model has five components: inputs, activities, outputs, outcomes, and impact. Let me explain each one in plain language.

Inputs are the resources you need to run the program. This includes money, staff, volunteers, equipment, space, partnerships, and anything else you need to get the work done. If Lisa's navigation program needs trained navigators, a phone system, an office, and a database of mental health providers, those are inputs.

Activities are what your program actually does—the specific actions your staff and volunteers carry out. For Lisa, activities include conducting intake assessments with families, matching families with appropriate providers, assisting with referral paperwork, making follow-up calls, and hosting community workshops.

Outputs are the direct, countable products of your activities. They measure how much you did. How many families received navigation services? How many referrals were made? How many workshops were held? How many people attended? Outputs tell you about volume and reach, but they don't tell you whether anything changed for the people you served.

Outcomes are the changes that happen as a result of your program. This is where it gets important. Outcomes measure what's different in people's lives because of your work. Did families actually connect with mental health services? Did the time between first contact and first appointment decrease? Did parents report feeling more confident navigating the system on their own? Did children's symptoms improve after receiving treatment? Outcomes are what funders, supporters, and your own conscience care about most.

Impact is the long-term, big-picture change your program contributes to. This is the broadest level of change and is often shared with other organizations and factors. For Lisa, impact might be a measurable reduction in emergency room visits for pediatric mental health crises in Franklin County, or an improvement in school attendance and academic performance among children who received timely mental health treatment. Impact takes years to measure and is influenced by many factors beyond your program, but it represents the ultimate goal of your work.

Lisa's Logic Model

HERE IS HOW LISA'S LOGIC MODEL LOOKED WHEN SHE PUT IT ALL TOGETHER:

Component	The Family Bridge Project
Inputs	Trained navigators, phone and computer equipment, office space, provider database, community partnerships with schools and churches, workshop materials, funding from grants and donations
Activities	Conduct intake assessments, match families with providers, assist with referral paperwork, make follow-up calls within two weeks, host monthly community workshops, maintain and update provider resource directory

Outputs	Number of families served, number of referrals made, number of follow-up calls completed, number of workshops held, number of workshop attendees, number of provider directory entries maintained
Short-Term Outcomes	Families connected to appropriate mental health provider within 30 days, families attend first appointment, parents report increased knowledge of children's mental health resources
Long-Term Outcomes	Children receiving consistent mental health services, families report improved family functioning, reduction in crisis-level mental health events among families served

Inputs Trained navigators, phone and computer equipment, office space, provider database, community partnerships with schools and churches, workshop materials, funding from grants and donations

Activities Conduct intake assessments, match families with providers, assist with referral paperwork, make follow-up calls within two weeks, host monthly community workshops, maintain and update provider resource directory

Outputs Number of families served, number of referrals made, number of follow-up calls completed, number of workshops held, number of workshop attendees, number of resource directories distributed

Outcomes Families connected with mental health services within 30 days, reduced time from first contact to first appointment, increased parent confidence in navigating services, improved child mental health symptoms after treatment

IMPACT REDUCED PEDIATRIC MENTAL HEALTH EMERGENCY ROOM VISITS IN

Franklin County, improved school attendance and academic performance among children receiving timely treatment, reduced stigma around seeking mental health support ———— ——————— ————————

This logic model tells a clear story. Resources go in, activities happen, countable things are produced, people's lives change, and the community gets better. Every element connects to the next. If you can build a logic model for your program, you've a blueprint that guides your work, explains your approach to funders, and gives you a framework for measuring your success.

DESIGNING YOUR PROGRAM STEP BY STEP

Now let me walk you through the practical process of designing a program from the ground up. Think of this as a six-step recipe.

STEP ONE: NAME THE CHANGE YOU WANT TO SEE

Start at the end. What is different in someone's life after they participate in your program? This is your desired outcome, and everything else flows backward from it. Do not start with what you want to do. Start with what you want to be true for the people you serve after you've done it. Lisa's desired outcome was clear: families would be connected with appropriate mental health services for their children within thirty days of contacting the organization. That specific, measurable outcome anchored her entire program design.

STEP TWO: IDENTIFY THE BARRIERS STANDING IN THE WAY

What prevents your target population from already being where you want them to be? These barriers are the things your program must address. If there were no barriers, there would be no need for your organization. Lisa identified three barriers: lack of knowledge about available services, a confusing and bureaucratic referral process, and stigma. Each barrier became a target for a specific program activity.

STEP THREE: CHOOSE ACTIVITIES THAT ADDRESS EACH BARRIER

For each barrier, design a specific activity or set of activities. The key is intentionality. Every activity in your program should exist because it directly addresses a documented barrier. If an activity doesn't connect to a barrier, ask yourself why you're doing it. Lisa's navigation service addressed the knowledge and bureaucracy barriers. Her community workshops addressed the stigma barrier. Nothing in her program was there just because it seemed like a nice idea. Every piece had a purpose.

STEP FOUR: DEFINE HOW YOU WILL DELIVER THE PROGRAM

Get specific about logistics. Where will the program take place? What days and hours will you operate? How will people access your services? What staff or volunteers do you need? What training do they require? What materials or equipment are necessary? The more detailed you're at this stage, the smoother your launch will be. Lisa decided that her navigation program would operate out of a donated office at a local community center, with navigators available by phone and in person Monday through Friday from nine in the morning to seven in the evening, and Saturdays from ten to two.

Workshops would be held monthly at rotating community locations to reach different neighborhoods.

STEP FIVE: DETERMINE WHAT YOU WILL MEASURE

We are going to go deep on measurement in the next section, but at the design stage, you need to identify what data you'll collect. This includes both outputs and outcomes. Decide now, before you launch, what information you'll track and how you'll collect it. If you wait until after you've been running for six months to think about data, you'll have missed valuable information that you can't go back and recapture.

STEP SIX: BUILD IN A PROCESS FOR LEARNING AND IMPROVING

No program is perfect on day one. The best organizations build regular review points into their program design—times when they step back, look at the data, listen to feedback from participants and staff, and ask what's working and what needs to change. Lisa planned quarterly reviews where she and her navigators would look at the numbers, discuss challenges they were encountering, and identify adjustments to improve the program. This isn't a sign of weakness. It is a sign of a mature, well-run organization.

MEASURING OUTCOMES: HOW TO KNOW IF YOUR PROGRAM IS WORKING

This is the section that separates organizations that survive from organizations that thrive. Measuring outcomes isn't just something funders require—although they do. It is something you need for yourself and for the people you serve. If you can't demonstrate that your program is making a real difference, you've no way of knowing whether to continue, expand, adjust, or start over. Measurement isn't a burden. It is a compass.

Let me be clear about the difference between outputs and outcomes, because this trips up a lot of people. Outputs tell you what you did. Outcomes tell you what changed. If you run a tutoring program, the number of tutoring sessions you held is an output. Whether students' reading scores improved is an outcome. If you run a food pantry, the number of families who received food boxes is an output.

Whether families reported less food insecurity three months later is an outcome. Outputs are necessary—you need to track them, and funders want to see them. But outcomes are what matter most because they tell you whether your work is actually making a difference.

TYPES OF OUTCOMES

Outcomes generally fall into three categories based on the timeline over which they occur. Short-term outcomes are changes you expect to see relatively quickly, often within days or weeks of someone participating in your program. For Lisa, a short-term outcome was that a family received a referral to a mental health provider within one week of their intake assessment.

Medium-term outcomes take longer to develop, usually weeks to months. For Lisa, a medium-term outcome was that the family actually attended their first appointment and began receiving services within thirty days.

Long-term outcomes are the deeper, more lasting changes that happen over months or years. For Lisa, long-term outcomes included improvement in the child's mental health symptoms, improved school attendance, and increased parent confidence in navigating healthcare systems independently.

You don't need to measure every possible outcome. Focus on a manageable number—two to four—that are most closely tied to your program's core purpose and that you can realistically track with your resources.

PRACTICAL TOOLS FOR MEASURING OUTCOMES

You don't need expensive software or a research team to measure your outcomes. Here are practical, accessible methods that any small nonprofit can use.

PRE AND POST SURVEYS

One of the simplest and most effective measurement tools is a survey given before and after someone participates in your program. The survey asks the same questions at both points, and you compare the answers to see if anything changed. For a mental health navigation program, a pre-survey might ask parents to rate their knowledge of available mental health services on a scale of one to five, their confidence in navigating the referral process on a scale of one to five, and their level of stress about their child's situation on a scale of one to five.

After the family has been connected with services and received a follow-up, the same questions are asked again. If the average knowledge score went from two to four, that's a measurable outcome you can report.

Keep surveys short—five to ten questions maximum. Use simple language. Offer the survey in the languages your participants speak. And make completing the survey as easy as possible—paper forms, online forms, or even verbal responses that your staff can record.

TRACKING LOGS AND DATABASES

A basic tracking system that records each participant's journey through your program is essential. This doesn't need to be a sophisticated database. A well-organized spreadsheet can work beautifully for a small organization. For each family Lisa served, her navigators recorded the date of first contact, the results of the intake assessment, which provider the family was referred to, whether the referral paperwork was completed, the date of the first scheduled appointment, whether the family attended the appointment, and the results of the two-week follow-up call.

This data allowed Lisa to calculate concrete outcomes: what percentage of families were connected with services within thirty days, what percentage actually attended their first appointment, and what the average time was from first contact to first appointment.

PARTICIPANT FEEDBACK AND TESTIMONIALS

Numbers tell part of the story. People's words tell the rest. Building regular opportunities for participant feedback into your program gives you qualitative data that brings your outcomes to life. This can be as simple as a brief follow-up conversation where you ask: How was your experience with our program? What was most helpful? What could we've done better? Would you recommend us to another family?

With permission, participant testimonials become powerful tools for fundraising, grant applications, and community presentations. When Lisa could say that eighty-five percent of families were connected with services within thirty days and then share a mother's story about how the program changed her family's life, the combination of numbers and narrative was compelling beyond anything either could achieve alone.

EXTERNAL DATA SOURCES

Some outcomes can be measured using data that already exists. If your program aims to improve school attendance, you can partner with the local school district to track attendance data for the children you serve. If your program aims to reduce emergency room visits, you might work with a hospital to access aggregate data. If your program addresses food insecurity, you can use the USDA's food security survey questions, which are publicly available, as a standardized measurement tool.

Using established data sources adds credibility to your outcomes because you're using tools and metrics that the broader field already recognizes.

SAMPLE OUTCOME MEASUREMENT FRAMEWORKS

Let me provide you with three complete examples of outcome measurement frameworks for different types of organizations so you can see how this works in practice.

EXAMPLE ONE: YOUTH MENTORING PROGRAM

Outcome	Measurement Tool	When Measured	Target
Mentees report increased self-confidence	Pre/post survey using 5-point scale	At enrollment and at 6 months	70% show improvement of 1+ points
Mentees improve school attendance	School attendance records	Quarterly, compared to prior year	80% maintain or improve attendance
Mentees demonstrate improved goal-setting skills	Goal tracking worksheet reviewed by mentor and staff	Quarterly	75% complete at least 2 of 3 set goals per quarter

TOOL**

Mentees report Pre/post survey At enrollment and 70% show increased using 5-point at 6 months improvement of 1+ self-confidence scale points

Mentees improve School attendance Quarterly, 80% maintain or school attendance records compared to prior improve year attendance

Mentor-mentee Program tracking Monthly check-ins 75% of matches matches sustain log complete the for full year school year ———–— — ——–— ———–— ———–--

EXAMPLE TWO: FOOD ASSISTANCE PROGRAM

Outcome	Measurement Tool	When Measured	Target
Families report reduced food insecurity	USDA 6-item food security survey	At intake and at 3 months	60% move to higher food security category
Families access additional food resources	Enrollment tracking for SNAP, WIC referrals	At each visit	40% enroll in at least one additional program
Families report improved dietary diversity	24-hour food recall survey	At intake and at 6 months	50% report increased fruit/vegetable consumption

TOOL**

Families report USDA 6-item food At intake and at 60% move to reduced food security survey 3 months higher food insecurity security category

Families access Enrollment At each visit 40% enroll in at additional food tracking for least one resources SNAP, WIC additional referrals program

Families report Post-workshop After each 80% report increased survey cooking class learning new knowledge of skills nutrition ———–— —— ——–— ———–— ———–--

EXAMPLE THREE: LISA'S MENTAL HEALTH NAVIGATION PROGRAM

Outcome	Measurement Tool	When Measured	Target
Families connected with provider within 30 days	Navigator tracking log	At 30-day follow-up	85% connected within 30 days
Families attend first appointment	Follow-up call confirmation	Within 2 weeks of scheduled appointment	75% attend first appointment

| Parents report increased understanding of child's mental health needs | Pre/post knowledge assessment | At intake and 3-month follow-up | 70% show measurable improvement |
| Families report satisfaction with navigation services | Client satisfaction survey | At case closure | 90% rate services as helpful or very helpful |

TOOL**

Families Navigator At 30-day 85% connected connected with tracking log follow-up within 30 days provider within 30 days

Families attend Follow-up call Within 2 weeks of 75% attend first first appointment confirmation scheduled appointment appointment

Parents report Pre/post survey, At intake and at 70% improve by 1+ increased 5-point scale 60-day follow-up points confidence navigating services

Workshop Post-workshop After each 80% report attendees report survey workshop increased comfort reduced stigma discussing mental health ———— ———— ———— ————

Each of these frameworks gives you a clear picture of what success looks like, how you'll know when you've achieved it, and what specific targets you're aiming for. When you write a grant application, these frameworks become the foundation of your evaluation plan. When you present to your board, these are the numbers you report on. When you need to make a decision about whether to continue, modify, or expand a program, these measurements give you the evidence to make an informed choice.

LEARNING FROM WHAT DOES NOT WORK

I want to spend time on something that most nonprofit books gloss over: what happens when your program doesn't work the way you expected. Because it will happen. I guarantee it. Some aspect of your program will fall flat. Some activity you were sure would be a hit won't resonate with participants. Some outcome target you set will seem laughably optimistic six months in. This isn't failure. This is learning.

Lisa experienced this firsthand. Her community workshops were one of the program components she was most excited about. She envisioned packed rooms, engaged parents, and transformative conversations about mental health. The reality was different. Her first workshop drew eight people. The second drew five. The third drew eleven, but most of them were service providers, not the parents she was trying to reach. Lisa was disappointed, but instead of giving up on workshops, she dug into the data and the feedback.

She asked the families who were using her navigation services why they hadn't attended the workshops. The answers were illuminating. Some parents didn't have childcare. Some couldn't get to the location. Several said they didn't want to attend something labeled as a "mental health workshop" because they were worried about being judged. Lisa used this feedback to redesign her workshops.

She moved them to schools where parents were already dropping off or picking up children. She provided childcare. She changed the name from "Mental Health Workshop" to "Family Wellness Night" and broadened the topics to include stress management, self-care, and parenting strategies alongside mental health resources. Attendance quadrupled.

That is what a healthy relationship with program evaluation looks like. You design the best program you can with the information you've. You launch it. You measure what happens. You listen to participants. And you adjust. The organizations that last aren't the ones that get everything right the first time. They are the ones that pay attention and keep improving.

PROGRAM DESIGN IS NEVER FINISHED

I want to make this point explicitly because it's easy to treat program design as a one-time exercise. You design the program, you launch it, and then you run it the same way forever. That approach will slowly kill your organization's effectiveness.

The communities you serve change. The problems you address evolve. New research emerges about what works. Your staff gain experience and insight that should inform how the program operates. The best nonprofit programs are living things—they grow, adapt, and improve over time based on evidence, feedback, and changing circumstances.

Build regular program review into your organizational calendar. At minimum, do a comprehensive review once a year where you look at all of your outcome data, gather feedback from participants and staff, compare your results to your targets, and identify specific changes to implement in the coming year. Quarterly check-ins on key metrics keep you on track between annual reviews.

Lisa made program review a standing agenda item at her quarterly board meetings. She presented the numbers: how many families served, what percentage connected with services within thirty days, what the average time to first appointment was, and what participants reported in their satisfaction surveys. The board asked questions, offered suggestions, and helped Lisa think through challenges. This regular rhythm of review and reflection kept the program sharp and gave the board meaningful, substantive work to engage with.

YOUR PROGRAMS ARE YOUR PROMISE

Everything in this book—the paperwork, the legal filings, the fundraising, the board meetings—exists to support the programs you deliver. Programs are your organization's promise to the community. When a family walks through your door or calls your phone number, they're trusting you with something precious: their hope that things can get better. Program design is how you honor that trust.

A well-designed program doesn't just happen. It is built intentionally, grounded in an understanding of the problem, informed by research and community input, structured with clear activities that address specific barriers, measured with practical tools, and refined through honest reflection on what works and what doesn't.

Take the time to build your logic model. Choose your outcome measurements. Set targets that are ambitious but realistic. Create systems for collecting data from day one. And embrace the reality that your program will evolve—because that evolution isn't a sign that you got it wrong. It is a sign that you're paying attention and committed to doing your best work.

In the next chapter, we're going to talk about money—how to fund the programs you've designed, where to find grants, how to approach donors, and how to build a financial foundation that keeps your organization sustainable. Great programs need resources, and the program design work you've done in this chapter will make you a far more compelling case for funding than any organization that can't articulate what it does, why it works, and how it knows.

Your programs are your legacy. Design them well.

The Regular Person Guide
CHAPTER 9: SETTING UP YOUR FINANCES

"A budget isn't a cage. It's a roadmap."

If the last chapter was about the heart of your organization—your programs—this chapter is about the engine that keeps that heart beating: your finances. I know this is the chapter some of you've been dreading. Money makes a lot of people uncomfortable, especially people who got into nonprofit work because they care about helping others, not crunching numbers.

If the word "budget" makes your palms sweat, I need you to stick with me. Because here's the truth: good financial management isn't separate from your mission. It is part of your mission. Every dollar that comes into your organization represents someone's trust—a donor's generosity, a funder's investment, a community's hope. Managing that money well is how you honor that trust.

The good news is that nonprofit finances, at least for a small, new organization, aren't nearly as complicated as you might think. You don't need an MBA. You don't need to become a certified public accountant. You need to understand some basic concepts, set up a few straightforward systems, and develop the habit of paying attention to where your money comes from and where it goes. This chapter is going to walk you through all of it, step by step, in the same plain English we've been using throughout this book.

OPENING YOUR ORGANIZATION'S BANK ACCOUNT

The very first financial step is opening a bank account in your organization's name. This might seem obvious, but I mention it because I've seen new founders make the mistake of running their nonprofit's money through their personal bank account. Do not do this. Ever. Mixing personal and organizational funds is one of the fastest ways to create a mess—legally, financially, and in terms of your credibility with donors and funders. From the very first dollar your organization receives, it should go into an account that belongs to the organization.

To open a nonprofit bank account, you'll need your organization's Employer Identification Number, which you obtained from the IRS. You will need a copy of your articles of incorporation. And you'll need a board resolution authorizing the opening of the account and designating who's signing authority. Most banks have experience setting up nonprofit accounts and will walk you through their specific requirements.

When choosing a bank, look for one that offers free or low-cost checking for nonprofits. Many banks and credit unions have specific nonprofit banking programs that waive monthly fees and minimum balance requirements. Ask about online banking features, which will make it much easier to track your transactions and reconcile your records. Also ask about the process for adding or changing signers on the account, since your board members may change over time.

Lisa opened her account at a local credit union that offered free nonprofit checking with no minimum balance. She set up the account with two authorized signers—herself as executive director and her board treasurer. The board passed a resolution requiring two signatures on any check over five hundred dollars, which is a common safeguard that protects against misuse of funds. The entire process took about forty-five minutes.

CHOOSING ACCOUNTING SOFTWARE

You need a system for tracking every dollar that comes in and every dollar that goes out. For a brand-new organization, this doesn't need to be anything fancy. But it does need to exist, and it needs to be organized from the start. Trying to reconstruct your financial records six months after the fact, when you suddenly need to file a tax return or report to a funder, is a nightmare you want to avoid.

There are several affordable options for small nonprofit accounting. QuickBooks Online offers a nonprofit version that many organizations use. Wave is a free accounting software that works well for very small organizations. Aplos is designed specifically for nonprofits and churches, with features for tracking donations and managing funds. For the very smallest organizations, even a well-organized spreadsheet can work in the first year, though I recommend moving to dedicated software as soon as your budget exceeds a few thousand dollars.

Whatever system you choose, make sure it can do a few essential things. It should be able to categorize income by source—donations, grants, event revenue, and so on. It should categorize expenses by type—salaries, rent, supplies, insurance, and other common categories. It should generate basic reports, especially a profit and loss statement and a balance sheet. And ideally, it should be able to track restricted funds separately from unrestricted funds, which brings us to one of the most important concepts in nonprofit finance.

RESTRICTED VERSUS UNRESTRICTED FUNDS: WHY THIS MATTERS

This is a concept that confuses a lot of new founders, but it's critically important, so let me explain it as clearly as I can. In the nonprofit world, not all money is created equal. Some money comes to you with strings attached, and some comes free and clear. Understanding the difference will save you from one of the most common and most serious financial mistakes a nonprofit can make.

Unrestricted funds are donations or revenue that you can use for any purpose that supports your mission. If someone writes a check to your organization with no special instructions, that money is unrestricted. You can use it to pay salaries, buy supplies, cover rent, or put it toward any legitimate organizational expense. Unrestricted funds are the most flexible and, frankly, the most valuable type of funding because they allow you to direct resources where they're needed most.

Restricted funds are money that comes with specific instructions from the donor or funder about how it must be used. If a foundation gives you a twenty-thousand-dollar grant to run your community workshops, that money is restricted to workshop expenses. You can't use it to pay your electric bill or buy office furniture, even if those things are desperately needed. If a donor gives you five hundred dollars and says, "I want this to go directly to helping families pay for their children's first therapy appointment," that money is restricted to that specific purpose.

Here is where people get into trouble. If you spend restricted funds on anything other than their designated purpose, you've violated the terms of the gift. This can result in having to return the money, losing future funding from that source, and serious damage to your organization's reputation. In extreme cases, misuse of restricted funds can lead to legal consequences. This isn't something to take lightly.

The practical implication is that you need to track restricted and unrestricted funds separately. When a grant comes in, record it as restricted to the specific purpose outlined in the grant agreement. When you spend money against that grant, record the expense against the restricted fund. At any given time, you should be able to tell your board, a funder, or an auditor exactly how much restricted money you've, what it's restricted to, and how much has been spent.

Lisa learned this lesson early when she received her first grant of fifteen thousand dollars from the county mental health board. The grant was specifically for navigator salaries and training. When her office computer broke and she needed a replacement, she was tempted to use some of the grant money to buy one. Instead, she checked the grant agreement, confirmed that equipment wasn't an allowable expense under the grant, and used unrestricted donation funds to replace the computer. It was the right call, and it protected her relationship with her funder.

WHAT FINANCIAL RECORDS TO KEEP

Good record-keeping isn't glamorous, but it's the backbone of financial accountability. Here is what you need to keep organized and accessible.

For every dollar that comes in, keep a record of who gave it, when they gave it, how much they gave, and whether it's restricted or unrestricted. For individual donations, this information is also essential for sending tax acknowledgment letters to your donors, which you're required to provide for any single gift of two hundred and fifty dollars or more.

For every dollar that goes out, keep the receipt or invoice, a record of what it was for, which budget category it falls under, and if applicable, which grant or restricted fund it was charged against. Get in the habit of keeping every receipt. If you pay for something with a credit card or debit card, save the receipt and match it to the transaction in your accounting system. If you write a check, record the check number, the payee, and the purpose.

Keep copies of all grant agreements, donor correspondence, bank statements, and financial reports. Most experts recommend keeping financial records for at least seven years, which is the general statute of limitations for IRS audits. Store physical records in a secure location and keep digital backups of everything.

Lisa set up a simple filing system with folders for bank statements, receipts organized by month, grant agreements, donor records, and annual financial reports. She spent about fifteen minutes each week entering transactions into her accounting software and reconciling them with her bank statement. It wasn't exciting work, but it gave her a clear, accurate picture of her organization's financial health at all times.

CREATING YOUR FIRST BUDGET

Now we get to the part that scares people the most, and I'm going to make it as painless as possible. A budget isn't a scary financial document created by accountants in dark rooms. A budget is a plan. It is your best estimate of how much money you expect to bring in over the next year and how you plan to spend it. That is all it's. If you've ever planned a family vacation by figuring out what it will cost and how you'll pay for it, you've already done a simplified version of budgeting.

Your budget has two sides: revenue, which is the money you expect to receive, and expenses, which is the money you expect to spend. The goal isn't to make these numbers perfectly equal—in fact, you want your revenue to be at least slightly higher than your expenses, because a small surplus gives you a cushion for unexpected costs and helps build a financial reserve over time.

THE REVENUE SIDE

Start by listing every source of income you expect for the year. For a new nonprofit, common revenue sources include individual donations from friends, family, and community supporters, grants from foundations or government agencies, fundraising events, corporate sponsorships, and program fees if you charge for any services. Be realistic. It is better to underestimate your revenue slightly and be pleasantly surprised than to overestimate and find yourself unable to cover your costs.

For each revenue source, write down the amount you reasonably expect to receive. If you've already received commitments or pledges, include those. If you plan to apply for grants, include only the ones you've a reasonable chance of receiving, and consider including them at a reduced amount to account for the possibility that you might not get the full award. If this is your first year and you've never raised money before, be conservative. You can always adjust your budget upward if more money comes in than expected.

The Regular Person Guide
THE EXPENSE SIDE

Now list everything you expect to spend money on. Nonprofit expenses generally fall into two broad categories: program expenses, which are costs directly related to delivering your services, and administrative expenses, which are the costs of running the organization itself.

Program expenses might include salaries for program staff, supplies and materials used in program delivery, transportation costs, venue rental for events or workshops, and training for staff and volunteers. Administrative expenses might include office rent, utilities, phone and internet service, insurance, accounting and legal fees, office supplies, website hosting, and bank fees.

There is also a third category that some organizations track separately: fundraising expenses. These include the costs of producing appeal letters, hosting fundraising events, purchasing donor management software, and similar costs associated with raising money.

When estimating costs you've never incurred before, there are a few practical approaches. Call vendors and get quotes. Ask other nonprofit leaders what they pay for similar expenses. Look online for typical costs in your area. And when in doubt, round up rather than down. Unexpected expenses always come up—a piece of equipment breaks, an insurance premium increases, a new regulatory requirement costs money to comply with. Building a cushion into your budget isn't pessimism. It is wisdom.

LISA'S FIRST-YEAR BUDGET

REVENUE

Revenue Source	Projected Amount
Individual Donations	$12,000
County Mental Health Board Grant	$20,000
Community Foundation Grant	$8,000
Corporate Sponsorships	$3,000
Fundraising Event	$2,000
Total Revenue	**$45,000**

EXPENSES

Expense Category	Projected Amount

Part-Time Navigator Salary	$18,000
Navigator Training	$1,500
Workshop Materials and Refreshments	$2,400
Office Supplies and Technology	$2,000
Insurance (General Liability)	$1,800
Phone and Internet Service	$1,200
Accounting and Legal Fees	$2,500
Website and Marketing	$1,500
Printing and Postage	$800
Fundraising Event Costs	$600
Miscellaneous and Contingency	$2,000
Total Expenses	**$34,300**

Projected Surplus (Reserve)	**$10,700**

Here is what Lisa's first-year budget looked like. Use this as a model for building your own.

REVENUE

EXPENSES

A few things to notice about Lisa's budget. First, her revenue exceeds her expenses, leaving a projected surplus of ten thousand seven hundred dollars. This is intentional. That surplus becomes the beginning of a financial reserve, which gives her organization a cushion if a grant comes in late, an unexpected expense arises, or revenue falls short in a given quarter. Building a reserve is one of the smartest financial moves a new nonprofit can make.

Second, Lisa included a miscellaneous and contingency line of two thousand dollars. This is money set aside specifically for expenses she can't predict. Something will come up that she didn't budget for. It always does. Having a contingency line means she doesn't have to panic or cut a program to cover it.

Third, Lisa's budget is modest and realistic. She isn't projecting a million-dollar operation in year one. She is planning for what she can reasonably raise and responsibly spend. Funders and board members respect a realistic budget far more than an ambitious one that the organization has no realistic path to achieving.

The Regular Person Guide

WHY BUILDING A FINANCIAL CUSHION MATTERS

I want to spend a moment on this because it's something that too many new nonprofits neglect. The nonprofit world is full of uncertainty. Grants get delayed. A major donor moves away. A fundraising event gets rained out. A global pandemic shuts everything down. If your organization is living paycheck to paycheck, any one of these events could be fatal.

Financial experts generally recommend that nonprofits work toward having three to six months of operating expenses in reserve. For a brand-new organization, that might seem impossibly ambitious. But you can start small. If your monthly expenses are three thousand dollars and you can save five hundred dollars a month, you'll have a three-month reserve within eighteen months. The point isn't to achieve the goal overnight but to build toward it consistently.

A financial reserve isn't hoarding money that should be spent on programs. It is responsible management that ensures your programs will still exist next year. Every dollar in reserve is a dollar of insurance against the unpredictable nature of nonprofit funding. Your board, your funders, and the families you serve are all better off when your organization has a financial safety net.

FINANCIAL TRANSPARENCY AND ACCOUNTABILITY

As a nonprofit, your organization's finances aren't private. You are stewards of public resources, and you've an obligation to be transparent about how you use them. This means presenting financial reports to your board at every meeting. It means filing your annual IRS return, known as Form 990, which becomes a public document that anyone can view. It means being prepared to answer questions from donors, funders, and the public about how you spend your money.

This transparency isn't something to fear. It is something to embrace. When you can show that every dollar is accounted for, that your spending aligns with your mission, and that you're building a financially healthy organization, you build trust. Trust leads to more funding, stronger partnerships, and a better reputation in your community.

Lisa presented a simple financial summary at every board meeting. It showed how much money came in that month, how much went out, what the bank balance was, and how the year-to-date actuals compared to the budget. It took her about thirty minutes to prepare and ten minutes to present. But it gave her board confidence that the organization's finances were in good shape, and it demonstrated the kind of accountability that funders look for when deciding where to invest their money.

COMMON FINANCIAL MISTAKES TO AVOID

Before we close this chapter, let me flag some of the most common financial mistakes I see new nonprofits make so you can steer clear of them.

The first is mixing personal and organizational funds. I mentioned this earlier, but it bears repeating. The moment you deposit a donation into your personal checking account or pay a personal expense from the organization's account, you've created a problem. Keep everything separate. Always.

The second is failing to track restricted funds properly. If a funder gives you money for a specific purpose and you can't show that you spent it on that purpose, you'll lose that funder and potentially face legal consequences. Track restricted funds from the moment they arrive to the moment they're fully spent.

The third isn't having a budget at all. Some new founders operate purely on instinct, spending money as it comes in without any plan for how it should be allocated. This approach works until it doesn't, which is usually the moment a large bill arrives or a major expense catches you off guard. A budget takes a few hours to create and saves you from countless sleepless nights.

The fourth is being afraid to spend money. This sounds counterintuitive, but some founders are so worried about running out of money that they refuse to invest in things the organization genuinely needs. They avoid hiring staff when the workload clearly demands it. They skip essential insurance. They use outdated equipment that slows down their work. Being frugal is wise. Being so cautious that your programs suffer isn't. Your budget should reflect the real costs of doing your work well.

The fifth is ignoring financial problems and hoping they'll resolve themselves. If your expenses are exceeding your revenue, or if a major funding source falls through, deal with it immediately. Adjust your budget. Reduce spending. Accelerate your fundraising. Talk to your board. Financial problems that are caught early can almost always be managed. Financial problems that are ignored become crises.

MONEY SERVES THE MISSION

I want to close with a reminder that reframes everything we've discussed in this chapter. Money isn't the point of your nonprofit. It is the fuel. Your mission is the point. Your programs are the vehicle. Money is what keeps the vehicle running so it can get where it needs to go. Managing it well isn't about becoming a finance expert. It is about honoring the trust that donors, funders, and your community have placed in you.

If you set up a proper bank account, choose a simple accounting system, understand the difference between restricted and unrestricted funds, keep clean records, and create a realistic budget with some cushion built in, you're ahead of a significant number of small nonprofits. These aren't complex tasks. They are habits—habits that, once established, take very little time to maintain and pay enormous dividends in terms of accountability, credibility, and organizational health.

In the next chapter, we're going to talk about fundraising—how to actually bring money into your organization. The financial systems you set up in this chapter will ensure that when the money starts flowing, you're ready to manage it responsibly and transparently. The people who believe in your mission are trusting you with their generosity. Show them that trust is well placed.

Now go open that bank account.

The Regular Person Guide
CHAPTER 10: FINDING FUNDING

"Fundraising isn't begging. It's inviting people to join a cause that
MATTERS."*

We need to have an honest conversation about money. Not about budgets and bank accounts—we covered that in the last chapter. This conversation is about where the money comes from, how you ask for it, and why so many nonprofit founders would rather do almost anything else than fundraise. If the thought of asking someone for money makes your stomach churn, you're in very good company. Fundraising is the number one source of anxiety for new nonprofit leaders, and it's the reason many promising organizations never reach their potential.

But here's what I need you to hear, and I need you to really let it sink in: fundraising isn't begging. It isn't charity in the shameful sense of the word. It isn't putting yourself in a position of weakness and hoping that someone with more money than you takes pity on your cause. Fundraising is an invitation. It is the act of offering people an opportunity to be part of something meaningful—something they care about but might not have the time, skills, or proximity to do themselves.

When you ask someone to support your organization, you're not taking from them. You are giving them a chance to make a difference.

That shift in mindset is the single most important thing I can teach you about fundraising. Once you internalize it, everything else becomes easier. Not easy—but easier. This chapter is going to walk you through the entire fundraising landscape, from individual donations to foundation grants to corporate partnerships and beyond. We will cover how to make your first ask, how to follow up without being annoying, how to show gratitude that keeps people giving, and why putting all your eggs in one funding basket is a recipe for disaster.

By the end, you'll have a practical, approachable plan for bringing money into your organization.

UNDERSTANDING THE FUNDRAISING LANDSCAPE

Before we get into tactics, let me give you the big picture. Nonprofit revenue comes from several different sources, and understanding each one—its advantages, its limitations, and how it fits into your overall strategy—is essential to building a sustainable organization.

INDIVIDUAL DONATIONS

Individual giving is the single largest source of charitable revenue in the United States. Every year, individuals give more to nonprofits than foundations, corporations, and government agencies combined. This is important because many new founders fixate on grants and ignore individual donors, which is like ignoring the ocean while searching for a swimming pool.

Individual donations come in all sizes, from five dollars to five million dollars. For a new organization, most of your individual giving will come in smaller amounts from people who know you personally—friends, family, coworkers, neighbors, and community members who believe in what you're doing. As your organization grows and builds a track record, you'll begin to attract larger gifts from people who may not know you personally but are passionate about your mission.

The beauty of individual giving is that it's almost always unrestricted. When someone writes a check to your organization because they believe in your work, that money can go wherever you need it most. That flexibility is incredibly valuable, especially in the early years when your needs are unpredictable and your funding sources are limited.

FOUNDATION GRANTS

Foundations are organizations that exist specifically to give money to nonprofits. They come in many sizes, from small family foundations that give away ten thousand dollars a year to massive national foundations that distribute billions. Foundation grants are typically larger than individual gifts and are almost always restricted to specific programs or purposes.

The grant application process can be competitive and time-consuming. Most foundations have specific areas of focus—mental health, education, poverty, the arts—and they receive far more applications than they can fund. Getting a foundation grant requires research to identify the right foundations, a well-written application that aligns your work with the foundation's priorities, and patience, because the process from application to decision can take months.

For new organizations, local and regional foundations are often the best starting point. Community foundations, which exist in most metropolitan areas, specifically support local nonprofits and often have grant programs designed for newer or smaller organizations. Your state's nonprofit association or your local United Way can help you identify foundations that might be a fit for your work.

GOVERNMENT FUNDING

Federal, state, and local government agencies provide billions of dollars in funding to nonprofits each year, primarily through grants and contracts. Government funding can be substantial—some organizations receive the majority of their revenue from government sources. However, government funding comes with significant reporting requirements, strict rules about how the money can be spent, and a level of bureaucratic complexity that can be challenging for small organizations.

For most brand-new nonprofits, government funding isn't realistic in the first year. Government funders typically want to see an established track record, financial stability, and the administrative capacity to manage complex grants. That said, it's worth learning about government funding opportunities in your area so you can position your organization to pursue them as you grow. Many local government entities, like county mental health boards or city community development offices, have smaller grant programs that are more accessible to newer organizations.

CORPORATE PARTNERSHIPS

Businesses support nonprofits in many ways: financial sponsorships, in-kind donations of goods or services, employee volunteer programs, and cause-related marketing partnerships. Corporate giving tends to be most accessible at the local level. The national headquarters of a large corporation might be hard to reach, but the local branch manager, franchise owner, or small business down the street is often very open to supporting community organizations.

When approaching businesses, think about what you can offer in return. Most corporate giving isn't purely altruistic—businesses want visibility, positive community association, and employee engagement opportunities. If you can offer logo placement on your website, recognition at events, or volunteer opportunities that help companies fulfill their community service goals, you've a much stronger pitch than simply asking for a check.

FUNDRAISING EVENTS

Events—galas, walkathons, silent auctions, community dinners, golf tournaments—are a staple of nonprofit fundraising. They can be effective for raising money and building community awareness, but they're also enormously time-consuming and, if not managed carefully, can cost almost as much as they bring in.

My advice for new organizations: start simple. A community dinner at a church hall, a small silent auction with donated items, or a casual fundraising gathering at a supporter's home costs very little to produce and can raise meaningful money while building your donor base. Save the black-tie gala for when your organization is established enough to fill a ballroom. In the early years, events should be about connecting with people and sharing your story, with fundraising as an important but secondary goal.

EARNED INCOME

Some nonprofits generate revenue by selling products or services related to their mission. A job training program might operate a small business where trainees work and learn. A community health organization might charge sliding-scale fees for certain services. An arts nonprofit might sell artwork created in its programs. Earned income can be a valuable supplement to donations and grants, but it requires careful thought about pricing, market demand, and the balance between revenue generation and mission delivery.

For most new nonprofits, earned income isn't a significant revenue source in the first year or two. But it's worth considering as part of your long-term funding strategy, especially if your programs lend themselves to a fee-for-service model or if there's a natural product or service you could offer.

STARTING WITH WHAT YOU HAVE: YOUR PERSONAL NETWORK

Here is a truth that every nonprofit founder needs to accept: your first donors will be people who know you. Not people who know your organization—people who know you. Your family. Your friends. Your coworkers. Your neighbors. Your church community. Your college roommate. Your kid's soccer coach. In the early days, people don't give because they've thoroughly analyzed your organization's impact data. They give because they trust you, they believe in you, and they want to support something you care about.

This is perfectly okay. In fact, it's how the vast majority of nonprofits start. And it's nothing to be embarrassed about. The people who love you want to see you succeed. Giving them the opportunity to be part of your journey is a gift, not a burden.

Lisa's first fundraising effort was a letter. Not a fancy direct mail piece designed by a marketing firm. A personal letter, written from the heart, that she sent to about seventy-five people in her life. She told them about The Family Bridge Project—why she started it, what problem it addressed, and how it would help families in their community. She described her vision, shared a story about a family she had already helped during her volunteer work, and asked each person to consider making a donation to help launch the organization.

That letter raised four thousand two hundred dollars. Forty-one people responded with gifts ranging from ten dollars to five hundred dollars. More importantly, it accomplished something that no grant application could: it built a base of supporters who were personally invested in Lisa's success. Those forty-one people became her first ambassadors, spreading the word about The Family Bridge Project to their own networks.

Several of them later volunteered. A few introduced Lisa to other potential donors. One connected her with a foundation board member who eventually helped her secure her first major grant.

That is the power of starting with your personal network. The money matters, but the relationships matter more.

MAKING THE ASK: HOW TO ACTUALLY DO IT

This is the part where the rubber meets the road. You know who to ask. You believe in your cause. But when it comes time to actually open your mouth and ask someone for money, something seizes up inside you. You feel awkward. You feel pushy. You feel like you're imposing. Every fiber of your being wants to talk about anything else.

I understand that feeling, and I'm going to give you a framework that makes asking not only manageable but genuinely enjoyable. The framework has four parts: connect, share, invite, and respect.

CONNECT

Before you ask for anything, connect with the person on a human level. If it's someone you know well, this might be as simple as asking about their family or catching up on their life. If it's someone you're meeting for the first time, find common ground. The goal is to establish that this is a conversation between two people who care about something, not a sales transaction.

SHARE

Tell your story. Not a rehearsed elevator pitch. Your actual story. Why did you start this organization? What did you see that compelled you to act? What has happened since you began? Share a specific example of how your work has made a difference—a family you helped, a moment that reinforced why this matters. People give to stories, not statistics. The data matters and you should have it ready, but the story is what moves hearts and opens wallets.

Lisa found that the most powerful thing she could share wasn't a statistic about wait times for mental health services. It was the story of a mother who called her office in tears, saying she had been trying to get help for her son for eight months and had been turned away at every door. Lisa described how her navigator walked that mother through the process, found a provider who could see her son within two weeks, and followed up to make sure the appointment happened.

When Lisa told that story—with the mother's permission—potential donors leaned in. They could see the impact. They could feel it.

INVITE

Here is where you make the ask, and I want you to notice the word I'm using: invite. You aren't demanding. You aren't pressuring. You are inviting someone to participate in something meaningful. The language might sound like this: "I'd love for you to be part of what we're building. Would you consider making a gift to support our work?" Or: "We are trying to raise ten thousand dollars this year to fund our navigation program. A gift of any amount would make a real difference. Would you be willing to contribute?"

Be specific when you can. If you're meeting with someone you believe could give five hundred dollars, it's okay to say, "Would you consider a gift of five hundred dollars?" People appreciate knowing what's being asked of them. A specific ask is easier to respond to than a vague one. But if you're not sure what amount to suggest, asking for "a gift of any amount" is perfectly fine.

The most important thing is to actually ask. Do not dance around it. Do not talk for twenty minutes about your organization and then end the conversation without ever making a clear request. If you don't ask, the answer is always no.

RESPECT

When you make an ask, be prepared for any response. Some people will say yes immediately and enthusiastically. Some will say they need to think about it, which is completely reasonable. Some will say they can't give right now, which you should accept graciously and without pressure. And some will say no. That is their right, and it doesn't diminish your relationship or your cause.

Never pressure, guilt, or manipulate anyone into giving. Never make someone feel bad for declining. Thank them for their time regardless of their answer, and let them know that their support can take many forms—volunteering, spreading the word, attending an event. A person who says no to a donation today might become your biggest champion tomorrow.

FOLLOWING UP AND SHOWING GRATITUDE

Fundraising doesn't end when someone writes a check. In many ways, that's where it begins. How you follow up after a gift determines whether that person gives again, and repeat donors are the lifeblood of a sustainable nonprofit. Here is what follow-up should look like.

Send a thank-you within forty-eight hours of receiving a gift. Not a week later. Not when you get around to it. Within two days. For gifts of any size, a prompt, personal thank-you letter is essential. For larger gifts, a phone call from the executive director or board chair is appropriate and deeply appreciated. The thank-you should acknowledge the specific amount of the gift, express genuine gratitude, and describe the impact the gift will have. Do not use a generic form letter that says "Dear Friend." Use the person's name. Reference something specific about them or their gift if you can.

Beyond the initial thank-you, keep your donors informed about how their money is being used. Send periodic updates—quarterly or at minimum annually—that show the impact of their contributions. Share stories, statistics, and milestones. When you achieve something significant, like reaching your hundredth family served or securing a major grant, let your donors know. They are part of your team, and they want to know that their investment is making a difference.

Lisa created a simple system for donor stewardship. Every donor received a handwritten thank-you note within forty-eight hours. Donors who gave one hundred dollars or more received a personal phone call from Lisa. Every quarter, she sent a one-page update to all donors with a brief story about a family they had helped, key statistics from the quarter, and a thank-you for their ongoing support. At the end of the year, she sent an annual report that summarized the year's accomplishments and recognized all donors by name.

The result of this approach was remarkable. Of the forty-one people who gave in Lisa's first year, thirty-four gave again the following year. Several increased their gifts. Three of them told Lisa that her thank-you notes and updates were the best they had ever received from any nonprofit. That kind of stewardship doesn't cost money. It costs time and intention. And it pays for itself many times over.

GETTING STARTED WITH FOUNDATION GRANTS

Foundation grants can provide significant funding, but pursuing them effectively requires preparation and strategy. Here is how to approach the process.

First, do your research. Not every foundation is a match for your organization, and applying to the wrong ones wastes your time and theirs. Look for foundations whose stated priorities align closely with your mission. A foundation that funds environmental conservation isn't going to fund a youth mentoring program, no matter how good your application is. Use free resources like the Foundation Directory Online, your local community foundation's website, and your state's nonprofit association to identify foundations that fund work like yours in your geographic area.

Second, read the guidelines carefully. Every foundation publishes guidelines that describe what they fund, how much they give, what the application process looks like, and what the deadlines are. Follow these guidelines to the letter. If they ask for a two-page letter of inquiry, don't send a ten-page proposal. If they fund organizations with budgets under five hundred thousand dollars, don't apply if your budget is seven hundred thousand. Foundations receive hundreds of applications and will eliminate yours immediately if it doesn't follow their instructions.

Third, tell your story clearly and compellingly. A strong grant application does three things: it describes the problem in specific, local terms; it explains your solution with concrete details about what you do and how it works; and it demonstrates your ability to deliver on your promises by sharing your qualifications, your track record, and your plan for measuring outcomes. All the work you did in earlier chapters—defining your problem, describing your programs, building your logic model, setting up outcome measurements—flows directly into your grant applications.

Fourth, build relationships before you apply. Many foundations are more receptive to applications from organizations they've already heard of. Attend foundation-hosted events. Introduce yourself to program officers. Ask if you can schedule a brief informational call to learn more about their priorities. These conversations give you valuable insight into what the foundation is looking for, and they put a face and a story behind your eventual application.

Lisa identified three foundations that were strong fits for her work. Before applying, she called the program officer at each one, introduced herself and her organization, and asked if her work aligned with their funding priorities. Two of the three encouraged her to apply. The third told her honestly that they weren't currently funding navigation services, which saved Lisa the time of writing an application that would have been declined.

She applied to the two that showed interest, and one of them funded her for eight thousand dollars in her first year. That single phone call—the one that yielded a polite no—was just as valuable as the one that led to a yes, because it directed her energy where it would be most productive.

BUILDING CORPORATE PARTNERSHIPS

Corporate partnerships work best when they're mutually beneficial. A business isn't just a checkbook. It is a potential partner with resources, reach, and influence that can amplify your work in ways that go beyond money.

Start local and start small. Approach businesses that have a natural connection to your mission or your community. For Lisa, this meant reaching out to local pediatricians' offices, family-oriented businesses, and companies whose employees were parents of school-age children. She offered sponsors the opportunity to have their logo on her workshop flyers, recognition on her website, and a presence at community events. In return, she asked for financial contributions, in-kind donations like printing services and refreshments, and help spreading the word about her programs.

Her approach wasn't transactional. She didn't walk into businesses with a sponsorship brochure and a list of prices. She walked in with a story about families in the community who needed help and an invitation for the business to be part of the solution. Some businesses gave money. Others donated supplies or services. A local printing company offered to produce all of Lisa's workshop materials for free.

A coffee shop donated refreshments for every community event. A technology company gave her organization a refurbished laptop and printer. Each of these contributions had real value, and each business felt like a genuine partner in the work.

WHY FUNDING DIVERSIFICATION IS NOT OPTIONAL

I can't stress this enough: don't rely on any single source of funding. This is one of the most critical lessons in nonprofit sustainability, and organizations that ignore it are the ones that close their doors when a single grant doesn't get renewed or a major donor moves away.

LET ME TELL YOU ABOUT AN ORGANIZATION I WILL CALL SECOND CHANCE

Services. They ran a successful reentry program for people coming out of incarceration. For five years, they received eighty percent of their funding from a single state government contract. The program was well run, the outcomes were strong, and the funding seemed secure. Then the state had a budget crisis. The contract was cut by sixty percent with ninety days' notice.

Second Chance Services had no individual donor base, no foundation relationships, and no corporate partnerships to fall back on. Within six months, they had to lay off most of their staff and dramatically reduce their programs. An organization that had been thriving was suddenly fighting for survival.

That story isn't unusual. It plays out every year in communities across the country. The solution is diversification—building multiple streams of revenue so that if one decreases, the others can sustain you while you adapt.

A healthy funding mix for a small to mid-sized nonprofit might look something like this: thirty to forty percent from individual donations, twenty-five to thirty-five percent from foundation grants, fifteen to twenty percent from government funding, and ten to fifteen percent from corporate partnerships and events. The exact percentages will vary based on your mission, your community, and your organization's stage of development. What matters is that no single source accounts for more than about forty percent of your total revenue.

Building this diversification takes time. In your first year, your revenue might come almost entirely from individual donations and one or two small grants. That is normal. But from day one, you should be thinking about and working toward multiple revenue streams. Every year, your funding base should get a little broader, a little more diverse, and a little more resilient.

IT GETS EASIER: THE FUNDRAISING LEARNING CURVE

I want to be honest with you about something. Your first fundraising ask will probably be uncomfortable. Your second will be slightly less uncomfortable. By your tenth, you'll have found your rhythm. By your fiftieth, you'll wonder why you were ever nervous. Fundraising is a skill, and like any skill, it improves with practice.

The founders who become great fundraisers aren't the ones with the smoothest pitches or the fanciest events. They are the ones who genuinely believe in their cause and who have learned to communicate that belief in a way that resonates with others. They are the ones who listen to potential donors, understand what motivates them, and connect those motivations to the organization's work. They are the ones who follow up, say thank you, and treat every donor—regardless of the size of their gift—as a valued partner.

Lisa will tell you that her first fundraising letter was agonizing to write. She rewrote it five times. She almost didn't send it. When the first donation came in—twenty-five dollars from a coworker—she cried. Not because of the amount, but because someone believed in her enough to invest real money in her vision. That twenty-five dollars gave her the courage to make the next ask, and the next, and the next.

Two years later, Lisa hosted a community fundraising breakfast that drew one hundred and twenty people and raised eighteen thousand dollars in a single morning. She told the same kinds of stories she told in that first letter—real families, real challenges, real impact. The only difference was that now she had more stories to tell, more data to share, and more confidence in her voice. The discomfort she felt at the beginning had been replaced by a deep sense of purpose. She wasn't asking for money. She was building a movement.

CREATING YOUR FIRST FUNDRAISING PLAN

Before I let you go, I want you to create a simple fundraising plan for your first year. This doesn't need to be a sophisticated document. It is a one-page roadmap that answers four questions.

First, how much money do you need to raise? Look at the budget you created in Chapter 9. The total revenue figure is your fundraising target.

Second, where will the money come from? Break your target down by source. How much do you expect from individual donations? How much from grants? How much from events or corporate partnerships? Be realistic, and remember that individual giving should be a significant portion of your plan.

Third, what specific actions will you take? For individual giving, will you send a letter, make personal calls, or host a small gathering? For grants, which foundations will you apply to, and when are their deadlines? For corporate partnerships, which businesses will you approach and what will you offer them? Write down specific actions with specific timelines.

Fourth, who is responsible for what? If you've a board, assign fundraising tasks to specific people. Even if everyone is nervous about it, sharing the responsibility makes it manageable. Perhaps one board member hosts a small gathering at their home. Another introduces you to a business owner they know. Another helps you research foundation opportunities. Fundraising should never rest entirely on the founder's shoulders.

Lisa's first-year fundraising plan fit on one page. Her target was forty-five thousand dollars. Her plan called for a personal appeal letter to seventy-five contacts in September, applications to two foundation grants in October and November, outreach to five local businesses in January, a small community gathering hosted by a board member in March, and a year-end appeal letter in December. Each action had a person responsible and a deadline. The plan wasn't fancy, but it was specific, actionable, and achievable.

You Are Not Begging. You Are Building.

I want to leave you with this thought, because it's the one that will carry you through every uncomfortable moment, every declined ask, and every grant rejection you'll inevitably face. You aren't begging for money. You are building something that your community needs. Every person who gives to your organization—whether they give ten dollars or ten thousand dollars—is choosing to be part of that building. They are saying, with their wallet, that they believe in what you're doing and they want it to succeed.

That is a beautiful thing. It is a partnership. It is trust made tangible. And it's an honor to be on both sides of that exchange—the person who asks and the person who gives.

Fundraising will get easier. You will get better at telling your story. You will learn which approaches work and which ones don't. You will build relationships with donors who become loyal supporters for years. And someday, you'll look back at that first terrifying ask and smile, because it was the moment you started turning your vision into reality, one conversation at a time.

In the next chapter, we're going to talk about getting the word out—how to tell your story, build your brand, and make your community aware that your organization exists and is ready to help. The fundraising skills you develop in this chapter—storytelling, relationship-building, and the courage to ask—are the same skills that will make your marketing and outreach effective.

Now go write that first letter. Or make that first call. Or invite someone to coffee. The money is out there. The people who want to give are out there. They are just waiting for you to invite them in.

The Regular Person Guide
CHAPTER 11: BUILDING YOUR TEAM

"The strongest organizations are built by people who chose to show up."*

Up to this point, much of this book has focused on you—your idea, your mission, your paperwork, your budget. But no nonprofit succeeds as a one-person operation. At some point, and probably sooner than you think, you're going to need help. Real, reliable, consistent help from people who share your passion and are willing to give their time, their skills, and their energy to bring your mission to life.

For most new nonprofits, that help comes first in the form of volunteers. Volunteers are the backbone of the nonprofit sector. Millions of people across the country give their time freely to causes they believe in, and their contributions make it possible for organizations to serve communities that could never afford to pay for all the work that needs to be done. Learning how to find good volunteers, create meaningful experiences for them, and keep them coming back is one of the most important skills you'll develop as a founder.

But this chapter isn't just about volunteers. It is also about looking ahead to the day when your organization is ready to hire paid staff. That might be a year from now, or it might be five years from now. Either way, understanding what it takes to become an employer—and thinking honestly about whether and when you'll pay yourself—will help you build intentionally rather than scrambling to figure it out when the moment arrives.

FINDING GOOD VOLUNTEERS

The first question most founders ask is, "Where do I find volunteers?" The answer is simpler than you might expect: you find them in the same places you found your board members, your donors, and your community supporters. Volunteers are all around you. They are at your church, your kids' school, your neighborhood association, your workplace, and your social media networks. They are retirees looking for purpose, college students needing experience, professionals wanting to give back, and community members who care about the same issues you do.

The key to recruiting volunteers isn't casting the widest possible net. It is being clear about what you need and making it easy for people to say yes. Vague requests like "we need volunteers" don't work. Specific requests do. Instead of asking the universe for help, try something like: "We need three volunteers to help staff our community workshop on Saturday, March fifteenth, from nine in the morning to noon.

Tasks include setting up chairs, greeting families, and distributing resource packets. No experience needed." That kind of specificity tells a potential volunteer exactly what they're signing up for, how much time it will take, and what they'll be doing. It removes the uncertainty that keeps many people from stepping forward.

Lisa recruited her first volunteers through a combination of personal outreach and community posting. She asked her board members to each identify two people who might be interested in volunteering. She posted on neighborhood social media groups. She put up flyers at the library and the community center. And she spoke at a local church about her organization and the need for volunteers. Within a month, she had a list of fourteen people who had expressed interest. Not all of them ended up volunteering regularly, but enough did to give Lisa the support she needed to launch her programs.

SCREENING VOLUNTEERS: PROTECTING YOUR ORGANIZATION AND YOUR COMMUNITY

Not everyone who wants to volunteer is the right fit, and some roles require a higher level of screening than others. If your volunteers will be working directly with vulnerable populations—children, elderly individuals, people with disabilities, or anyone in a sensitive situation—you've a responsibility to screen them carefully.

At a minimum, every volunteer should complete a basic application that includes their contact information, relevant skills or experience, and references. For roles that involve direct contact with vulnerable populations, you should conduct background checks. Many states require background checks for anyone working with children, and even in states where it's not legally required, it's a best practice that protects the people you serve and reduces your organization's liability.

Background check services are available online at reasonable costs, typically twenty to fifty dollars per check. Some organizations that provide volunteer management resources, like VolunteerMatch or local volunteer centers, can help you navigate the screening process. Your insurance provider may also have requirements or recommendations about volunteer screening.

Lisa required all of her navigators—whether paid or volunteer—to complete an application, provide two references, and pass a background check. For volunteers who helped with events but didn't interact directly with families, she required an application and references but not a background check. This tiered approach balanced thoroughness with practicality. She was careful to explain to every volunteer why screening was important: not because she didn't trust them, but because the families they served needed to know that everyone in the organization had been vetted.

TRAINING VOLUNTEERS TO SUCCEED

One of the biggest mistakes new organizations make with volunteers is failing to train them properly. You can't hand someone a task they've never done before, offer no guidance, and then be frustrated when they do it poorly. Volunteers deserve the same investment in training that you'd give a paid employee, adjusted for the scope of their role.

Training doesn't have to be elaborate. For a volunteer helping set up chairs at an event, a five-minute walkthrough is probably sufficient. But for a volunteer navigator who will be interacting with families in crisis, training needs to be comprehensive. Lisa developed a twelve-hour training program for her volunteer navigators that covered the basics of children's mental health, how to conduct an intake assessment, how to use the provider database, confidentiality requirements, cultural sensitivity, and what to do in an emergency.

She spread the training over four three-hour sessions and required all navigators to complete it before they could work with families.

That investment in training paid dividends in multiple ways. Her volunteers felt confident and prepared, which made them more effective and more likely to stay. Families received a consistent, professional experience regardless of which navigator they worked with. And Lisa could trust that her volunteers were representing the organization well, which freed her to focus on other priorities instead of constantly supervising every interaction.

CREATING EXPERIENCES THAT KEEP VOLUNTEERS COMING BACK

Here is a truth about volunteers that every nonprofit leader needs to understand: people volunteer because they want to feel useful, connected, and appreciated. If your volunteer experience delivers those three things, people will keep coming back. If it doesn't, they'll quietly disappear, and you'll be constantly scrambling to replace them.

Making volunteers feel useful starts with giving them meaningful work. Nobody wants to show up and be handed busywork while the real action happens elsewhere. Match volunteers to tasks that matter and that use their strengths. If someone is a great writer, ask them to help with your newsletter. If someone is outgoing and warm, put them in a role where they interact with the public.

If someone is detail-oriented, give them data entry or record-keeping tasks. When people feel that their specific skills are valued and that their contribution makes a real difference, they're far more invested than when they're sweeping floors because nobody could think of anything else for them to do.

Making volunteers feel connected means including them in the community of your organization. Invite them to team meetings. Share updates about the organization's progress. Introduce them to each other. Create opportunities for social connection—a pizza lunch after a big event, a holiday appreciation gathering, a group outing. People stay with organizations where they feel like they belong, not where they feel like disposable labor.

Making volunteers feel appreciated is the easiest and most overlooked piece of the puzzle. Say thank you. Say it often. Say it specifically. Instead of a generic "thanks for volunteering," try "Thank you for helping Maria's family complete their intake paperwork yesterday. Your patience and kindness made a real difference during a stressful moment for them." Specific appreciation shows that you notice what they do and that it matters.

Other forms of recognition—volunteer of the month acknowledgments, annual appreciation events, handwritten notes, small tokens of gratitude—all reinforce the message that your volunteers are valued members of your team.

DEALING WITH COMMON VOLUNTEER CHALLENGES

Let's talk about some of the challenges that every organization faces when working with volunteers, because pretending these don't exist won't help you.

UNRELIABLE VOLUNTEERS

This is the number one frustration for nonprofit leaders who depend on volunteer labor. You plan an event around having six volunteers, and only three show up. A volunteer commits to a weekly shift and then stops coming without explanation. Someone enthusiastically signs up and then never follows through.

The reality is that volunteers are giving their time freely, and life happens. Kids get sick. Work schedules change. Enthusiasm fades. You can't demand reliability from unpaid helpers the way you can from employees. What you can do is set clear expectations from the beginning, follow up promptly when someone misses a commitment, and build redundancy into your plans.

If you need six volunteers for an event, recruit eight. If a critical role depends on one person, cross-train a backup. And when a volunteer is consistently unreliable, have a kind but honest conversation about whether this is still the right time for them to be involved.

THE FOUNDER WHO CANNOT LET GO

This challenge is about you, the founder, not about the volunteers. Many founders struggle to delegate because they believe no one can do the work as well as they can. They recruit volunteers and then hover over them, redo their work, or take tasks back when they're not done perfectly. This behavior exhausts the founder and demoralizes the volunteers. People who feel micromanaged and untrusted don't stick around.

If this sounds like you, hear me clearly: your volunteers don't need to do things exactly the way you'd do them. They need to do them well enough, and "well enough" might look different from your version of perfection. Your job as a founder is to set standards, provide training, and then step back and let people do the work. You will be amazed at how capable your volunteers are when you give them room to contribute in their own way.

Lisa caught herself doing this early on. She had trained a volunteer navigator and then found herself listening to every phone call the volunteer made, second-guessing the referrals, and adding notes to the paperwork. After a few weeks, the volunteer pulled her aside and said gently: "Lisa, I feel like you don't trust me to do this." That conversation was a turning point. Lisa apologized, committed to letting her volunteers work independently while remaining available for questions, and watched her team flourish as a result.

VOLUNTEER BURNOUT

Just because someone isn't being paid doesn't mean they can't burn out. Volunteers who take on too much, who are asked to fill gaps that should be covered by paid staff, or who feel like the organization would collapse without them are at high risk of exhaustion and resentment. Protect your volunteers by being honest about the scope of their roles, respecting their boundaries about how much time they can give, and recognizing when the workload has grown beyond what volunteers can reasonably handle. That recognition is often the signal that it's time to start thinking about hiring.

KNOWING WHEN YOU ARE READY TO HIRE

There comes a point in many organizations' growth when volunteers alone can't sustain the work. The volume of services has increased beyond what part-time, unpaid helpers can manage. Critical functions need someone who is available consistently, not just when they can fit it in around their day job. Quality and reliability require a level of accountability that's difficult to maintain with an all-volunteer workforce.

So how do you know when it's time to hire? Here are some signals to watch for. Your programs are growing, and you're turning people away because you don't have the capacity to serve them. Your volunteers are stretched thin and starting to burn out or drift away. You are spending so much time on administrative tasks that you can't focus on the mission-critical work.

Funders are asking about your staffing structure, and an all-volunteer operation is making them hesitant to invest. And you've enough consistent revenue—not just one-time windfalls, but reliable ongoing funding—to cover a salary and related costs for at least twelve months.

That last point is crucial. Do not hire someone unless you're confident you can pay them for at least a year. Bringing someone on board and then having to let them go three months later because the money ran out is devastating for the employee, disruptive for your programs, and damaging for your reputation. If you're not sure you can sustain a position, consider hiring on a part-time or contract basis first to test the waters.

WHAT POSITION TO FILL FIRST

When you're ready to make your first hire, the question is: what role will have the greatest impact? The answer depends on your organization's specific needs, but there are two common approaches.

The first approach is to hire for your core program. If your organization's primary service requires consistent, skilled delivery, your first hire might be a program coordinator or direct service provider. For Lisa, this meant hiring a part-time navigator—someone who could be available to families on a regular schedule and deliver the navigation services that were the heart of the organization's mission. This hire directly increased the number of families she could serve and improved the quality and consistency of the experience.

The second approach is to hire for administration. If you as the founder are drowning in bookkeeping, grant reporting, scheduling, and email while the mission-critical work suffers, your first hire might be an administrative assistant or office manager. This person handles the operational tasks that consume your time, freeing you to focus on programs, fundraising, and organizational leadership. A good administrative hire can be transformative for a founder who's been trying to do everything alone.

There is no universally right answer. Think about where the bottleneck is in your organization. What isn't getting done, or not getting done well, because you don't have the capacity? That is probably where your first hire should be.

The Regular Person Guide
THE BASICS OF BECOMING AN EMPLOYER

Hiring your first employee is exciting, but it also comes with a significant set of legal and administrative responsibilities. Let me walk you through the essentials so you know what's ahead.

PAYROLL

When you hire an employee, you become responsible for withholding federal income tax, Social Security tax, and Medicare tax from their paycheck, and remitting those withholdings to the IRS. You will also need to pay the employer's share of Social Security and Medicare, and you may owe state and local payroll taxes depending on where you're located. Additionally, you're typically required to carry workers' compensation insurance and pay into your state's unemployment insurance fund.

This sounds overwhelming, and if you try to manage it all manually, it can be. That is why I strongly recommend using a payroll service. Services like Gusto, ADP, or Paychex handle tax withholding, filing, and payments for you. They cost between thirty and seventy-five dollars per month for a small organization, and they save you from the headaches and penalties that come with making payroll tax mistakes. This isn't an area to cut corners. The IRS takes payroll tax obligations very seriously, and the penalties for errors can be severe.

EMPLOYMENT LAW

As an employer, you need a basic understanding of employment law. Federal laws like the Fair Labor Standards Act set minimum wage and overtime requirements. Anti-discrimination laws prohibit hiring or firing based on race, gender, religion, age, disability, and other protected characteristics. If you've employees, you need to comply with rules about workplace safety, employee records, and posting requirements. Your state likely has additional employment laws that may be more stringent than federal requirements.

You don't need to become an employment lawyer, but you do need to either educate yourself on the basics or consult with an attorney or human resources professional who can help you set up compliant practices from the start. Many state nonprofit associations offer employment law workshops and resources specifically for small organizations.

The Regular Person Guide

POLICIES YOU NEED

Before you bring on your first employee, you should have basic employment policies in place. At minimum, these should include a job description that clearly outlines the position's responsibilities and qualifications, an employee handbook or set of workplace policies covering attendance, conduct, leave, and grievance procedures, an at-will employment statement if your state follows at-will employment, and a process for performance evaluation.

These documents protect both the organization and the employee by setting clear expectations. They don't need to be lengthy or complicated, but they need to exist.

THE HONEST CONVERSATION: PAYING YOURSELF AS THE FOUNDER

This is the topic that many nonprofit books tiptoe around, so let me address it directly. If you're the founder and you plan to serve as the executive director of your organization, you're allowed to be paid for your work. A nonprofit isn't a vow of poverty. The prohibition on private benefit means that no one should be enriching themselves at the organization's expense, but it doesn't mean that the people who run the organization must work for free forever.

That said, the transition from unpaid founder to paid executive director requires careful handling. Here are the principles that should guide the process.

First, the decision to pay the founder must be made by the board of directors, not by the founder. You shouldn't set your own salary. That is a conflict of interest. The board should research comparable salaries for similar positions at similar organizations in your area and set compensation that's reasonable and justifiable. The IRS uses the concept of "reasonable compensation," which means the salary should be in line with what someone in a similar role at a similar organization would earn.

Second, the organization needs to be able to afford it. Paying yourself before the organization has stable, sufficient revenue to cover the cost is a recipe for financial problems. Many founders work unpaid for the first one to three years while the organization establishes itself and builds a funding base. Others start with a modest stipend and gradually increase their compensation as revenue grows. There is no single right timeline, but the principle is clear: the organization's financial health comes first.

Third, be transparent about it. Founder compensation should be disclosed in your IRS Form 990, which is a public document. There is nothing shameful about being paid for your work, but secrecy or evasiveness about compensation erodes trust. When Lisa's board determined that the organization was financially ready to pay her a part-time salary in the second year, they documented the decision in the board minutes, including the research they used to determine that the salary was reasonable.

Lisa included the compensation in her next annual report to donors. Nobody objected. In fact, several donors told her they were glad she was finally being compensated for the incredible amount of work she was doing.

The Regular Person Guide
CHAPTER 12: KEEPING IT GOING

"Starting is brave. Sustaining is where the real work begins."

Congratulations. If you've been reading this book from the beginning and doing the work along the way, you've accomplished something remarkable. You took an idea—a feeling, a frustration, a vision for something better—and you turned it into a real organization. You defined your mission, built your board, filed your paperwork, designed your programs, set up your finances, started raising money, and began building a team. That is no small thing. You should be proud.

But I need to be honest with you one more time, the same way I've been honest with you throughout this book: starting a nonprofit is the easy part. Keeping it going is where the real challenge begins. The excitement of launching fades. The daily grind of operations sets in. Problems arise that you didn't anticipate. The people and resources you counted on don't always come through. And the mission—the thing that drove you to start all of this—can get buried under paperwork, meetings, and the relentless demands of running an organization.

This final chapter is about sustainability in the deepest sense of the word. Not just financial sustainability, though we'll talk about that. But organizational sustainability—building something that's healthy enough, resilient enough, and well-managed enough to continue making a difference for years and even decades to come. We are going to cover the ongoing compliance requirements that keep your organization in good standing, the common challenges that derail nonprofits in their first few years, and the habits and practices that distinguish organizations that thrive from those that fade away.

STAYING IN COMPLIANCE: THE ONGOING REQUIREMENTS

Once your nonprofit is up and running, there are certain things you must do on a regular basis to maintain your legal status and stay in good standing with federal, state, and local authorities. Missing these requirements can result in penalties, loss of tax-exempt status, or even involuntary dissolution of your organization. None of that's as scary as it sounds, as long as you stay organized and keep track of your deadlines.

The most important ongoing requirement is filing your annual information return with the IRS. For most small nonprofits, this is either Form 990, Form 990-EZ, or Form 990-N, depending on your organization's gross receipts. Form 990-N, also called the e-Postcard, is for organizations with gross receipts of fifty thousand dollars or less. It is a very simple online filing that takes about five minutes.

Form 990-EZ is for organizations with gross receipts between fifty thousand and two hundred thousand dollars. Form 990 is the full return required for larger organizations. Your return is due on the fifteenth day of the fifth month after the end of your fiscal year. For most organizations that operate on a calendar year, that means May fifteenth.

This isn't optional. If your organization fails to file its annual return for three consecutive years, the IRS will automatically revoke your tax-exempt status. Getting it reinstated is possible but expensive and time-consuming. Put the filing deadline on your calendar, set reminders, and don't let it slip.

Beyond the IRS, you likely have state-level requirements as well. Most states require nonprofits to file an annual report with the Secretary of State's office, and many states require registration with the attorney general's charitable trust division or a similar agency, especially if you're soliciting donations from the public. Some states require you to renew your charitable solicitation registration annually. The fees and deadlines vary by state, so research your specific state's requirements and add every deadline to your compliance calendar.

Your board also has ongoing governance requirements. Your bylaws likely specify how often the board must meet, how minutes must be recorded, and when officer elections take place. Follow your bylaws. Hold your meetings. Keep your minutes. Elect your officers. These aren't just legal formalities—they're the practices that keep your organization accountable and well-governed.

YOUR ANNUAL COMPLIANCE CALENDAR

Here is a sample compliance calendar that you can customize for your organization. Adjust the specific months based on your fiscal year and your state's requirements.

Month** **Task** **Filed With

JANUARY REVIEW PRIOR YEAR FINANCES; INTERNAL BEGIN PREPARING ANNUAL RETURN

February Send donor acknowledgment Donors letters for prior year gifts (for tax purposes)

March Hold annual board meeting; elect Internal (record in officers; approve budget for new minutes) fiscal year

April Finalize annual return (Form Internal review 990, 990-EZ, or 990-N); review with board treasurer

MAY FILE IRS ANNUAL RETURN (DUE MAY IRS 15 FOR CALENDAR-YEAR ORGANIZATIONS)

June File state annual report (check Secretary of State your state's specific deadline)

July Mid-year financial review with Internal (board meeting) board; compare actuals to budget

August Review and update insurance Insurance provider policies; renew as needed

SEPTEMBER BEGIN PLANNING YEAR-END INTERNAL FUNDRAISING CAMPAIGN

October Renew charitable solicitation Attorney General / State registration (check your state's Agency deadline)

November Conduct annual program review; Internal (board meeting) evaluate outcomes data

December Year-end fundraising appeal; Donors / Public prepare annual report for donors and community ———- —————————-- —— ——————

Print this calendar, customize it for your state and fiscal year, and post it somewhere you'll see it regularly. Lisa kept hers on the wall next to her desk with check marks next to each item as she completed it. It took the anxiety out of compliance by turning it into a routine instead of a series of surprises.

THE CHALLENGES THAT SINK NONPROFITS IN THEIR FIRST FIVE YEARS

Research consistently shows that a significant number of new nonprofits don't survive beyond their first five years. The ones that close their doors aren't always the ones with the weakest missions or the worst ideas. Often, they're organizations led by passionate people who were blindsided by challenges they didn't see coming. I want you to see them coming. Here are the most common ones.

FOUNDER BURNOUT

This is the silent killer of new nonprofits. The founder pours every ounce of energy into the organization—working nights, working weekends, sacrificing personal relationships, ignoring their own health—and eventually hits a wall. They become exhausted, resentful, and unable to function at the level the organization needs. When the founder burns out, the organization often burns out with them, because everything was built around one person's unsustainable effort.

I've seen this happen to talented, dedicated people, and it breaks my heart every time. The antidote isn't working harder. It is building systems that distribute the workload, delegating to your board and your team, setting boundaries around your time, and taking care of yourself with the same intentionality you bring to taking care of your community. You aren't serving your mission by running yourself into the ground. You are serving your mission by building an organization that doesn't depend on any one person working eighty hours a week.

Lisa was honest with herself about this risk. She set a personal rule: no nonprofit work after eight o'clock on weeknights and no work on Sundays. She didn't always stick to it perfectly, but having the boundary meant she caught herself before she went too far. She also made a point of telling her board when she was feeling overwhelmed, which allowed them to step in and share the load rather than leaving her to carry everything alone.

BOARD CONFLICTS

A dysfunctional board can destroy an organization from the inside. Conflicts between board members, between the board and the founder, or between factions with different visions for the organization's future can paralyze decision-making, drive away donors and supporters, and create a toxic environment that no one wants to be part of.

The best defense against board conflict is prevention. Set clear expectations from the beginning, as we discussed in Chapter 5. Use your bylaws as a framework for resolving disputes. Address small disagreements before they become big ones. And remember that healthy disagreement is different from destructive conflict. A board where everyone always agrees isn't a strong board. A board where people can disagree respectfully, discuss their differences openly, and commit to a decision once it's made—that's a strong board.

If a board conflict does arise that can't be resolved through normal channels, don't let it fester. Bring in a neutral third party—a nonprofit consultant, a mediator, or a respected community leader—to help facilitate a resolution. The cost of outside help is always less than the cost of letting a conflict tear your organization apart.

FUNDING GAPS

Money problems are the most obvious threat to organizational survival. A major grant doesn't get renewed. A key donor stops giving. A fundraising event falls short of its goal. Revenue drops while expenses stay the same, and suddenly the organization is operating in the red.

We talked about funding diversification in Chapter 10, and this is where that strategy pays off. An organization with five revenue sources can survive the loss of one. An organization with one or two revenue sources might not. Beyond diversification, the financial reserve we discussed in Chapter 9 is your emergency fund. Three to six months of operating expenses in the bank gives you time to adjust, pivot, and find new revenue without having to slash programs or close your doors.

When a funding gap does hit—and at some point, it will—act fast. Cut non-essential expenses immediately. Accelerate your fundraising efforts. Be transparent with your board about the situation and involve them in developing a recovery plan. Do not hide financial problems or hope they'll resolve themselves. They won't.

SCOPE CREEP

Scope creep is what happens when an organization gradually takes on more and more activities that are outside its original mission. It usually starts innocently. A family asks for help with something your organization doesn't currently address, and you want to help, so you say yes. A funder offers money for a program that's tangentially related to your mission, and the money is too good to pass up, so you take it on. A board member has a great idea for a new initiative, and it sounds exciting, so you add it to your plate.

Before you know it, your organization is doing twelve things instead of three, none of them particularly well, and your staff and volunteers are stretched so thin that the core programs—the ones that define your mission—are suffering. Scope creep dilutes your impact, confuses your community about what you do, and exhausts your resources.

The cure for scope creep is your mission statement. Every time someone suggests a new activity, program, or direction, hold it up against your mission and ask: does this directly advance the work we were created to do? If the answer is yes, consider it carefully. If the answer is no, say no—graciously, but firmly. Your mission statement isn't just a sentence on your website. It is a filter that protects your organization from distraction.

Lisa faced this temptation in her second year when a local school asked if her organization could start providing after-school tutoring for children whose mental health challenges had caused them to fall behind academically. It was a real need, and Lisa cared about those kids. But tutoring wasn't her mission. Mental health navigation was. She referred the school to an existing tutoring organization and stayed focused on what The Family Bridge Project did best.

That discipline allowed her to go deeper and serve more families within her core mission rather than spreading thin across multiple programs.

WHAT SEPARATES THE ORGANIZATIONS THAT THRIVE

After years of working with nonprofits, I've observed that the organizations that make it past the five-year mark and go on to do transformative work in their communities share certain qualities. These aren't secrets. They are habits and values that anyone can cultivate.

The first quality is clarity of mission. Thriving organizations know exactly who they serve, what they do, and why it matters. Their mission isn't a vague aspiration. It is a sharp, focused commitment that guides every decision. When a thriving organization says no to something outside its mission, it does so confidently, because it knows that focus is what makes impact possible.

The second quality is strong governance. Thriving organizations have engaged, responsible boards that provide real oversight, make thoughtful decisions, and hold the organization accountable. The board and the executive director have a healthy, transparent relationship built on mutual respect. Governance isn't treated as a chore but as the foundation of organizational integrity.

The third quality is financial discipline. Thriving organizations live within their means, build reserves, diversify their funding, and manage their money with transparency and accountability. They don't chase every dollar. They pursue funding that aligns with their mission and that they can manage responsibly.

The fourth quality is a commitment to learning. Thriving organizations measure their outcomes, listen to the people they serve, and continuously improve their programs based on evidence. They aren't afraid to admit when something isn't working. They treat failure as information, not as shame.

The fifth quality is leadership depth. Thriving organizations don't depend on a single person. They develop leaders at every level—board members, staff, and volunteers who are invested in the mission and capable of carrying it forward. When the founder eventually steps back, the organization doesn't collapse. It continues, because the mission has been woven into the fabric of the organization itself, not just into the energy of one individual.

WHAT SUSTAINABILITY REALLY MEANS

Sustainability is a word that gets thrown around a lot in the nonprofit world, usually in reference to money. Can the organization sustain its funding? But real sustainability is much broader than finances. It is about building an organization that's healthy in every dimension—financially, programmatically, governmentally, and culturally—so that the mission can continue regardless of any single person's involvement.

True sustainability means that if you, the founder, had to step away tomorrow for any reason—illness, family obligations, a career change, retirement—the organization could continue without you. That might feel like a distant concern right now, but it's something you should be building toward from day one. Document your processes. Share institutional knowledge. Develop your board's capacity to lead. Invest in the skills and leadership of your staff and volunteers. Build an organization, not a personal project.

Lisa thought about this from the very beginning. She didn't want The Family Bridge Project to be "Lisa's organization." She wanted it to be the community's organization. She documented every process—how navigators conducted intakes, how workshops were planned, how grants were tracked, how donors were acknowledged. She cross-trained her team so that multiple people could handle each function. She shared decision-making authority with her board and her staff. And she talked openly about the future, including the day when she would no longer be at the helm.

By her fourth year, The Family Bridge Project had served over five hundred families. It had a budget of one hundred and twenty thousand dollars, a part-time staff of three, a dedicated volunteer corps of twenty-five, and a board of seven committed leaders. But the most important measure of Lisa's success wasn't any of those numbers. It was the fact that the organization could function without her in the room. That was sustainability. That was the goal all along.

ONE LAST WORD

We started this book with you sitting with an idea and a lot of uncertainty. Maybe you were at your kitchen table, or on your couch, or riding the bus home from work, turning over a thought that wouldn't leave you alone. Something in your community was broken, and something inside you said, "I could do something about this."

You have done something about it. You have taken that idea and given it a name, a mission, a legal structure, a board, a set of programs, a budget, a team, and a plan for the future. You have joined a long tradition of ordinary people who decided that the problems they saw weren't someone else's responsibility—they were theirs. And by taking that responsibility, you've created something that has the power to change lives.

The road ahead won't be smooth. There will be days when the paperwork is overwhelming, when the money is tight, when a program doesn't work the way you planned, when a board member frustrates you, when a funder says no, and when you wonder if any of it's worth the effort. On those days, I want you to remember why you started. Go back to the napkin, the notebook, the conversation that sparked this whole thing. Remember the problem you saw and the people you wanted to help. They are still there. They still need what you're building.

Starting a nonprofit is one of the hardest things you'll ever do. It is also one of the most meaningful. You are creating something that serves people who might otherwise be overlooked. You are building a bridge between a problem and a solution. You are proving that one person with a clear idea and a willing heart can make a real, lasting difference.

I'm proud of you for getting this far. Now go keep it going.

The community is counting on you.

The Regular Person Guide
APPENDICES

Practical Tools and Resources to Supplement Each Chapter

The Regular Person Guide

APPENDIX A: SAMPLE ARTICLES OF INCORPORATION

Note: This is a sample template for educational purposes. Requirements vary by state. Consult your state's Secretary of State website and consider having an attorney review your documents before filing.

ARTICLES OF INCORPORATION
OF
_____, INC.
A Nonprofit Corporation

Article I – Name

The name of this corporation shall be _____, Inc. (hereinafter referred to as the "Corporation").

Article II – Duration

The period of duration of the Corporation shall be perpetual.

Article III – Purpose

This Corporation is organized exclusively for charitable and educational purposes within the meaning of Section 501(c)(3) of the Internal Revenue Code of 1986, as amended, or the corresponding provision of any future federal tax law.

Specifically, the Corporation is organized to _____.

Notwithstanding any other provision of these Articles, the Corporation shall not carry on any other activities not permitted to be carried on by a corporation exempt from federal income tax under Section 501(c)(3) of the Internal Revenue Code, or by a corporation contributions to which are deductible under Section 170(c)(2) of the Internal Revenue Code.

Article IV – Prohibited Activities

No part of the net earnings of the Corporation shall inure to the benefit of, or be distributable to, its directors, officers, or other private persons, except that the Corporation shall be authorized and empowered to pay reasonable compensation for services rendered and to make payments and distributions in furtherance of the purposes set forth herein.

No substantial part of the activities of the Corporation shall be the carrying on of propaganda, or otherwise attempting to influence legislation, and the Corporation shall not participate in, or intervene in (including the publishing or distribution of statements), any political campaign on behalf of or in opposition to any candidate for public office.

Article V – Dissolution

Upon the dissolution of the Corporation, its assets remaining after payment of, or provision for payment of, all liabilities and obligations of the Corporation shall be distributed for one or more exempt purposes within the meaning of Section 501(c)(3) of the Internal Revenue Code, or the corresponding section of any future federal tax code, or shall be distributed to the federal government, or to a state or local government, for a public purpose.

Article VI – Registered Agent

The name and address of the initial registered agent of the Corporation is: _____, _____

Article VII – Incorporator

The name and address of the incorporator is: _____, _____

Article VIII – Board of Directors

The Corporation shall be governed by a Board of Directors. The number of directors shall be fixed by the Bylaws of the Corporation but shall be no fewer than _____ and no more than _____.

The names and addresses of the initial Board of Directors are:

_____, _____
_____, _____
_____, _____

Article IX – Limitation of Liability

To the fullest extent permitted by law, no director of the Corporation shall be personally liable to the Corporation for monetary damages for breach of fiduciary duty as a director.

_____

Signature of Incorporator: _____

Date: _____

Printed Name: _____

The Regular Person Guide
APPENDIX B: SAMPLE BYLAWS TEMPLATE

Note: This is a sample template for educational purposes. Customize for your organization's specific needs and state requirements. Consider having an attorney review your bylaws before adoption.

BYLAWS OF _____, INC.

Article I – Name and Office

Section 1.1. Name. The name of the Corporation shall be _____, Inc.

Section 1.2. Principal Office. The principal office of the Corporation shall be located at _____, or at such other place as the Board of Directors may designate from time to time.

Article II – Purpose

Section 2.1. The Corporation is organized and shall be operated exclusively for charitable and educational purposes as described in Section 501(c)(3) of the Internal Revenue Code. Specifically, the Corporation shall _____.

Article III – Board of Directors

Section 3.1. General Powers. The business and affairs of the Corporation shall be managed by its Board of Directors.

Section 3.2. Number. The Board of Directors shall consist of no fewer than _____ and no more than _____ directors.

Section 3.3. Election and Term. Directors shall be elected by a majority vote of the existing Board of Directors. Each director shall serve a term of _____ years. Directors may serve no more than _____ consecutive terms. After a one-year absence, a former director may be re-elected.

Section 3.4. Staggered Terms. The initial Board of Directors shall divide terms so that approximately one-third of the directors' terms expire each year, ensuring continuity of governance.

Section 3.5. Vacancies. A vacancy on the Board may be filled by a majority vote of the remaining directors. A director appointed to fill a vacancy shall serve for the remainder of the unexpired term.

Section 3.6. Removal. A director may be removed by a two-thirds vote of the remaining directors if the director (a) misses three consecutive meetings without prior notice; (b) engages in conduct detrimental to the Corporation; or (c) fails to fulfill the duties of a director. The director shall be given written notice and an opportunity to be heard before a vote on removal.

Section 3.7. Compensation. Directors shall not receive compensation for their service as directors but may be reimbursed for reasonable expenses incurred in the performance of their duties.

Article IV – Meetings of the Board

Section 4.1. Regular Meetings. The Board of Directors shall hold no fewer than _____ regular meetings per year at such times and places as the Board may determine.

Section 4.2. Special Meetings. Special meetings may be called by the Chair or by any _____ directors upon _____ days' written notice to all directors.

Section 4.3. Notice. Written notice of each meeting shall be provided to all directors at least _____ days in advance, specifying the date, time, location, and agenda.

Section 4.4. Quorum. A majority of the directors then in office shall constitute a quorum for the transaction of business.

Section 4.5. Voting. Each director shall have one vote. Unless otherwise specified in these Bylaws, decisions shall be made by a majority vote of directors present at a meeting where a quorum exists.

Section 4.6. Remote Participation. Directors may participate in meetings by telephone or video conference, provided all participants can hear and communicate with each other.

Section 4.7. Action Without a Meeting. Any action that may be taken at a meeting of the Board may be taken without a meeting if a written consent setting forth the action is signed by all directors.

Article V – Officers

Section 5.1. Officers. The officers of the Corporation shall be a Chair (or President), a Vice Chair (or Vice President), a Secretary, and a Treasurer.

Section 5.2. Election and Term. Officers shall be elected by the Board of Directors at the annual meeting for a term of _____ years and may serve consecutive terms.

Section 5.3. Chair. The Chair shall preside at all meetings of the Board and serve as the primary liaison between the Board and the Executive Director.

Section 5.4. Vice Chair. The Vice Chair shall perform the duties of the Chair in the Chair's absence and shall assist the Chair as needed.

Section 5.5. Secretary. The Secretary shall be responsible for recording minutes of all Board meetings, maintaining the Corporation's official records, and ensuring that proper notice is given for all meetings.

Section 5.6. Treasurer. The Treasurer shall oversee the Corporation's financial affairs, ensure that accurate financial records are maintained, present financial reports to the Board at each regular meeting, and ensure that the annual IRS return is filed on time.

Article VI – Committees

Section 6.1. The Board of Directors may establish standing committees and ad hoc committees as it deems necessary. Committee members shall be appointed by the Chair with Board approval.

Section 6.2. Committees shall make recommendations to the full Board. No committee shall have the authority to take final action unless specifically authorized by the Board.

Article VII – Executive Director

Section 7.1. Appointment. The Board of Directors may appoint an Executive Director who shall be responsible for the day-to-day management of the Corporation's affairs.

Section 7.2. Duties. The Executive Director shall implement the policies and programs established by the Board, manage staff and volunteers, oversee financial operations, and represent the Corporation to the public.

Section 7.3. Compensation. The Executive Director's compensation shall be determined by the Board of Directors based on comparable compensation for similar positions and the Corporation's financial capacity.

Article VIII – Fiscal Year

Section 8.1. The fiscal year of the Corporation shall begin on January 1 and end on December 31 of each year, unless otherwise determined by the Board of Directors.

Article IX – Conflict of Interest

Section 9.1. The Corporation shall adopt and maintain a Conflict of Interest Policy requiring directors, officers, and key employees to disclose any actual or potential conflicts of interest and to recuse themselves from decisions in which they have a personal or financial interest.

Article X – Amendments

Section 10.1. These Bylaws may be amended by a two-thirds vote of the Board of Directors at any regular or special meeting, provided that the proposed amendment has been distributed to all directors in writing at least _____ days prior to the meeting.

Article XI – Dissolution

Section 11.1. The Corporation may be dissolved by a two-thirds vote of the Board of Directors. Upon dissolution, all remaining assets shall be distributed in accordance with Article V of the Articles of Incorporation and Section 501(c)(3) of the Internal Revenue Code.

Adopted by the Board of Directors on: _____

Chair Signature: _____

Date: _____

Secretary Signature: _____

Date: _____

The Regular Person Guide

APPENDIX C: FORM 1023 WALKTHROUGH WITH SAMPLE RESPONSES

Note: This walkthrough is based on the major sections of IRS Form 1023. The IRS may update the form periodically. Always use the most current version from IRS.gov. The sample responses below use the fictional "Family Bridge Project" as an example.

Part I: Identification of Applicant

This section asks for basic information about your organization. Complete every field carefully and double-check for accuracy.

What to include:

- Full legal name exactly as it appears on your Articles of Incorporation
- Mailing address (use the organization's address, not a personal address if possible)
- Employer Identification Number (EIN) — apply at IRS.gov if you have not already
- Date incorporated and state of incorporation
- Contact person name, phone number, and email

Part II: Organizational Structure

Attach copies of your Articles of Incorporation and Bylaws. The IRS will review them for required language. Make sure your articles include:

- An exempt purpose clause referencing Section 501(c)(3)
- A dissolution clause directing assets to another 501(c)(3) or government entity
- A clause prohibiting private inurement (no profits to individuals)

Part IV: Narrative Description of Activities

This is the most important section. Describe every activity your organization conducts or plans to conduct. Be specific and concrete.

Sample Response — The Family Bridge Project:

> "The Family Bridge Project operates a family mental health navigation program serving Franklin County, Ohio. Our primary activity is connecting families with affordable mental health services for their children ages 5–18.
>
> When a family contacts our organization by phone, email, or walk-in referral, a trained navigator conducts an intake assessment (approximately 30–45 minutes) to understand the family's needs, including the child's symptoms, the family's insurance status, prior attempts to access services, and any barriers such as transportation or language.
>
> The navigator then searches our provider database to identify mental health professionals who accept the family's insurance or offer sliding-scale fees. The navigator assists the family with completing referral paperwork, scheduling appointments, and arranging transportation through partnerships with local transit services. Within two weeks of the referral, the navigator contacts the family to confirm the appointment was kept and services are underway.
>
> Additionally, the organization hosts monthly community workshops at schools, churches, and community centers. These free workshops educate parents about children's mental health, reduce stigma, and inform families about available resources. We also maintain and distribute a printed and online resource directory of local mental health providers, support groups, and crisis services.

All services are provided at no cost to families. The program is staffed by one part-time paid navigator and four trained volunteer navigators, supervised by the Executive Director."

Part V: Compensation and Financial Arrangements

Sample Response:

"The Executive Director receives an annual salary of $_____, which was determined by the Board of Directors based on salary surveys of comparable positions at similar-sized nonprofits in the region. One part-time navigator receives an hourly wage of $_____ for approximately 20 hours per week. No directors receive compensation for their board service. All compensation decisions are documented in Board meeting minutes."

Part IX: Financial Data

Provide actual financial data for any completed fiscal years and projections for the current year plus two future years. The IRS wants to see that your projected revenue and expenses are reasonable and consistent with your described activities.

Tips for Financial Projections:

- Revenue and expenses should be in the same general range — large gaps raise questions
- Show modest, realistic growth rather than wildly optimistic projections
- Make sure spending categories align with the activities you described in Part IV
- If relying heavily on grants not yet received, note them as "projected" and explain your basis for the estimate
- Include a narrative explanation of any unusual items or significant assumptions

APPENDIX D: FIRST-YEAR BUDGET TEMPLATE

Customize this template for your organization. Replace the sample amounts with your own realistic estimates. Your budget should reflect the true costs of operating your programs and the revenue sources you have identified.

Revenue

Revenue Source	Projected Amount	Notes
Individual Donations	$_____	Friends, family, community
Foundation Grant #1	$_____	Name: _____
Foundation Grant #2	$_____	Name: _____
Government Grant	$_____	Agency: _____
Corporate Sponsorships	$_____	
Fundraising Events	$_____	
Earned Income / Fees	$_____	
Other Revenue	$_____	
TOTAL REVENUE	**$_____**	

Expenses — Program

Expense Category	Projected Amount	Notes
Program Staff Salaries	$_____	
Payroll Taxes and Benefits	$_____	Approx. 15–20% of salaries
Program Supplies and Materials	$_____	
Training Costs	$_____	Staff and volunteer training
Event / Workshop Expenses	$_____	Venue, food, materials
Transportation	$_____	Mileage, client transport
Subtotal — Program	**$_____**	

Expenses — Administrative

Expense Category	Projected Amount	Notes
Rent / Office Space	$_____	
Utilities / Phone / Internet	$_____	
Insurance	$_____	General liability, D&O
Accounting and Legal Fees	$_____	Annual filing, bookkeeping
Office Supplies and Technology	$_____	
Website and Marketing	$_____	
Printing and Postage	$_____	
Fundraising Expenses	$_____	Event costs, appeals
Miscellaneous / Contingency	$_____	5–10% of total budget
Subtotal — Administrative	**$_____**	

TOTAL EXPENSES		$_____
PROJECTED SURPLUS / (DEFICIT)		$_____

Budget Approved by Board of Directors on: _____

Treasurer Signature: _____

APPENDIX E: BOARD MEMBER AGREEMENT TEMPLATE

This agreement is not a legal contract but a statement of mutual expectations between the organization and its board members. It helps ensure that everyone understands their role and commitment from the start.

BOARD MEMBER AGREEMENT

_____, Inc.

I, _____, understand that as a member of the Board of Directors of _____, I have a legal and ethical responsibility to ensure that this organization does the best work possible in pursuit of its mission. I believe in the mission of the organization and will act responsibly and prudently as its steward.

As a board member, I commit to the following:

Governance and Attendance
- I will attend at least _____% of regular board meetings each year.
- I will come prepared to meetings by reviewing the agenda and supporting materials in advance.
- I will actively participate in discussions and decision-making.
- I will serve on at least one committee and contribute to its work.

Fiduciary Responsibility
- I will exercise the duty of care by staying informed about the organization's activities and acting in good faith.
- I will exercise the duty of loyalty by putting the organization's interests ahead of my personal interests.
- I will exercise the duty of obedience by ensuring the organization follows its mission and complies with all applicable laws.
- I will disclose any conflicts of interest promptly and recuse myself from related decisions.

Financial Support
- I will make a personal financial contribution to the organization each year at a level that is meaningful to me.
- I will actively participate in fundraising activities, which may include making personal asks, hosting events, thanking donors, or identifying potential supporters.

Ambassadorship
- I will represent the organization positively in the community.
- I will help identify and recruit potential board members, volunteers, and partners.
- I will keep board discussions and sensitive organizational information confidential.

Term of Service
My term of service shall be _____ years, beginning on _____ and ending on _____. I understand that I may be asked to serve an additional term at the end of this period.

If I am unable to fulfill these commitments, I will proactively discuss the situation with the Board Chair and, if necessary, offer my resignation so that another committed person may serve.

Board Member Signature: _____

Date: _____

Printed Name: _____

Board Chair Signature: _____

Date: _____

Printed Name: _____

The Regular Person Guide
APPENDIX F: CONFLICT OF INTEREST POLICY

The IRS expects 501(c)(3) organizations to maintain a conflict of interest policy. This template covers the essential elements.

CONFLICT OF INTEREST POLICY

_____, Inc.

Article I – Purpose

The purpose of this Conflict of Interest Policy is to protect the interests of _____, Inc. (the "Organization") when it is contemplating entering into a transaction or arrangement that might benefit the private interest of a director, officer, or key employee. This policy is intended to supplement, not replace, any applicable state and federal laws governing conflicts of interest.

Article II – Definitions

Interested Person: Any director, officer, or key employee who has a direct or indirect financial interest, as defined below, is an interested person.

Financial Interest: A person has a financial interest if the person has, directly or indirectly: (a) an ownership or investment interest in any entity with which the Organization has a transaction or arrangement; (b) a compensation arrangement with the Organization or with any entity or individual with which the Organization has a transaction or arrangement; or (c) a potential ownership or investment interest in, or compensation arrangement with, any entity or individual with which the Organization is negotiating a transaction or arrangement.

Article III – Procedures

Duty to Disclose. Any interested person must disclose the existence and nature of their financial interest to the Board of Directors before any relevant discussion or vote.

Determining Whether a Conflict Exists. After disclosure, the Board shall determine whether a conflict of interest exists. The interested person may present information but shall leave the meeting during the discussion and vote on the matter.

Addressing the Conflict. If a conflict exists, the Board shall determine by a majority vote of the disinterested directors whether the transaction or arrangement is in the Organization's best interest, is fair and reasonable, and whether the Organization can obtain a more advantageous arrangement with reasonable efforts. The Board shall make its decision and document it in the minutes.

Violations. If the Board has reasonable cause to believe that a person has failed to disclose an actual or potential conflict of interest, it shall inform the person and allow them to explain. If the Board determines a violation has occurred, it shall take appropriate corrective action.

Article IV – Annual Statements

Each director, officer, and key employee shall annually sign a statement affirming that they have received a copy of this policy, have read and understood it, and agree to comply with it. The statement shall also require disclosure of any known financial interests that could give rise to a conflict.

Article V – Records

The minutes of the Board shall contain the name of the person who disclosed the conflict, the nature of the conflict, any action taken to determine whether a conflict existed, the Board's decision, and the names of those present for the discussion and vote.

Annual Disclosure Statement

I have received, read, and understand the Conflict of Interest Policy of _____, Inc. I agree to comply with this policy.

I have the following potential conflicts of interest to disclose (or "None"):

_____

_____

Signature: _____

Date: _____

Printed Name: _____

Position: _____

The Regular Person Guide

APPENDIX G: ANNUAL COMPLIANCE CALENDAR

Customize this calendar for your state and fiscal year. Add specific deadlines, responsible persons, and check boxes to track completion. This assumes a January–December fiscal year.

Month	Task	Filed With	Completed
January	Review prior year finances; begin preparing annual return	Internal	☐
February	Send donor acknowledgment letters for prior year gifts	Donors	☐
March	Hold annual board meeting; elect officers; approve new budget	Internal (minutes)	☐
April	Finalize annual return; review with board treasurer	Internal review	☐
May	File IRS annual return (Form 990/990-EZ/990-N) — due May 15	IRS	☐
June	File state annual report (check your state's deadline)	Secretary of State	☐
July	Mid-year financial review with board; compare actuals to budget	Board meeting	☐
August	Review and renew insurance policies	Insurance provider	☐
September	Begin planning year-end fundraising campaign	Internal	☐
October	Renew charitable solicitation registration (check state deadline)	Attorney General	☐
November	Conduct annual program review; evaluate outcomes data	Board meeting	☐
December	Year-end fundraising appeal; prepare annual report	Donors / Public	☐

Additional State-Specific Deadlines:

_____

_____

_____

APPENDIX H: GLOSSARY OF TERMS IN PLAIN ENGLISH

This glossary defines common nonprofit terms in the same plain language used throughout this book. Keep it handy as a reference.

501(c)(3): A section of the IRS tax code that grants tax-exempt status to organizations operating for charitable, educational, religious, scientific, or similar purposes. When people say "nonprofit," they usually mean a 501(c)(3).

Articles of Incorporation: The legal document filed with your state that officially creates your nonprofit corporation. Think of it as your organization's birth certificate.

Board of Directors: The group of people who govern your nonprofit. They set the organization's direction, approve the budget, hire the executive director, and ensure the organization follows its mission and the law.

Bylaws: The internal rules that govern how your organization operates—how the board meets, how decisions are made, how officers are elected, and similar matters. Bylaws are not filed with the state but are legally binding on your organization.

Charitable Solicitation Registration: A registration required by many states before you can legally ask the public for donations. Requirements and fees vary by state.

Conflict of Interest: A situation where a board member, officer, or employee has a personal or financial interest that could influence their decision-making on behalf of the organization.

Determination Letter: The official letter from the IRS confirming that your organization has been granted 501(c)(3) tax-exempt status. Keep this letter forever—you will need it for grant applications, banking, and other purposes.

Dissolution Clause: Language in your Articles of Incorporation that describes what happens to the organization's assets if it shuts down. The IRS requires that assets go to another 501(c)(3) or a government entity.

Donor Acknowledgment Letter: A written thank-you sent to donors that includes the amount of their gift and a statement that no goods or services were provided in exchange (or describes what was provided). Required by the IRS for gifts of $250 or more.

Duty of Care: The legal obligation of board members to be reasonably informed, participate actively, and make thoughtful decisions. In plain English: pay attention and take your role seriously.

Duty of Loyalty: The legal obligation of board members to put the organization's interests above their own. No self-dealing, no conflicts of interest, no using the organization for personal gain.

Duty of Obedience: The legal obligation of board members to ensure the organization follows its mission and complies with all laws and its own governing documents.

Earned Income: Revenue that a nonprofit generates by selling products or services, as opposed to receiving donations or grants.

EIN (Employer Identification Number): A unique nine-digit number assigned by the IRS to identify your organization for tax purposes. It is like a Social Security number for your nonprofit.

Executive Director: The person hired by the board to manage the nonprofit's day-to-day operations. In a new organization, the founder often serves as the executive director.

Fiscal Sponsorship: An arrangement where an established nonprofit provides legal and financial oversight for a project or new organization that does not yet have its own 501(c)(3) status.

Fiscal Year: The twelve-month period used for budgeting and financial reporting. Many nonprofits use the calendar year (January through December), but you can choose a different twelve-month period.

Form 990: The annual information return that most tax-exempt organizations must file with the IRS. It reports the organization's finances, governance, and activities and is available to the public.

Form 1023: The full IRS application for 501(c)(3) tax-exempt status. Requires detailed information about your organization's structure, programs, and finances.

Form 1023-EZ: A simplified version of the IRS application for smaller organizations (generally those with projected annual gross receipts of $250,000 or less).

Grant: Funding provided by a foundation, government agency, or corporation for a specific purpose. Grants usually come with requirements about how the money can be spent and what reports you must submit.

In-Kind Donation: A non-cash contribution of goods or services, such as donated office supplies, professional services provided for free, or use of a meeting space at no charge.

Logic Model: A visual tool that maps how your program works: what resources you put in, what activities you do, what you produce, and what changes as a result.

Mission Statement: A clear, concise statement of what your organization does, who it serves, and why it matters. It is the most important sentence your organization will ever write.

Outcomes: The changes that happen in people's lives as a result of your program. Unlike outputs (which count what you did), outcomes measure what is different because of what you did.

Outputs: The direct, countable products of your program activities—number of people served, workshops held, referrals made, meals distributed.

Private Inurement: The prohibited practice of using a nonprofit's resources to benefit individuals, such as directors or officers, beyond reasonable compensation.

Public Charity: The most common type of 501(c)(3) organization, funded by a broad base of public support including individual donations, grants, and government funding.

Quorum: The minimum number of board members who must be present at a meeting for the board to conduct official business. Usually a simple majority of the total board.

Reasonable Compensation: Salary and benefits that are comparable to what similar organizations pay for similar work.

Registered Agent: A person or company designated to receive legal documents on behalf of your organization. Required in every state where you are incorporated.

Restricted Funds: Donations or grants that come with specific instructions about how they must be used. You cannot spend restricted money on anything other than its designated purpose.

Scope Creep: The gradual expansion of an organization's activities beyond its original mission, usually driven by good intentions but resulting in diluted impact and stretched resources.

Social Enterprise: A business that exists primarily to address a social problem, generating revenue through products or services while prioritizing mission impact over profit.

Tax-Deductible Donation: A gift to a 501(c)(3) organization that the donor can claim as a deduction on their federal income taxes, reducing their taxable income.

Tax-Exempt Status: Recognition by the IRS that your organization does not owe federal income tax on revenue related to its mission. Does not exempt you from all taxes—payroll taxes and some others still apply.

Unrestricted Funds: Donations or revenue that can be used for any purpose that supports the organization's mission. The most flexible and often most valuable type of funding.

Vision Statement: A description of the future your organization is working to create. While the mission describes what you do now, the vision describes the world you are trying to build.

www.ingramcontent.com/pod-product-compliance
Lightning Source LLC
Chambersburg PA
CBHW020656300426
44112CB00007B/403